D1527691

Oscar Israelowitz's

GUIDE TO THE

JEWISH

WEST

Israelowitz Publishing

P.O.Box 228   Brooklyn, New York 11229   Tel. (718) 951-7072

CONTENTS

Introduction

This third volume of the series, *Guide to Jewish U.S.A.*, explores the growth and development of the Jewish communities of the Western states. The first Jewish communities developed directly as a result of the discovery of gold in California in 1848. Jews followed the gold mining camps and set up stores which sold clothing, mining equipment and food to the miners. There is a section devoted to Jewish historic sights in the old Gold Rush towns.

Several pioneer Jews were involved in politics. The first Jewish governor in the country, Moses Alexander, was elected governor of Idaho in 1914. Many other Jews were elected as mayors and city councilmen.

The motion picture industry in Hollywood was started by Jesse Lasky and Samuel Goldwyn in 1913 when they produced their first full-length production called *The Squaw Man*. The first "talkie" motion picture, *The Jazz Singer*, was produced in 1927 and starred the Jewish actor, Al Jolson. Today, many Jews hold leading positions in the movie, television and music industry.

This guide contains the vital information required for the Jewish traveler such as kosher restaurants, synagogues, mikvehs and eruvs. There is also information about Jewish historic landmarks, ancient cemeteries and museums. There is a section devoted to Jewish singles and where to find places to go Israeli folk dancing.

For the general traveler, there is information about all of the museums in the major cities and towns, places to take the kids, going house-hunting in Beverly Hills, where to go hot air ballooning and whitewater rafting, where to find ancient volcanoes and lava beds, and even where to go prospecting for gold!

ALASKA

Alaska, the 49th State, possesses a unique and colorful history which has been greatly enriched by its Jewish residents. The first were among the Vitus Bering expedition, which is credited for chartering the waters of Alaska in 1741.

The Jewish-owned Alaska Commercial Company held sole rights from 1867 to 1890 to take seals in the Pribilof Islands for fur trading. Responsible for popularizing the use of sealskins, the company developed a steamboat transportation system to ship ice to San Francisco, financed Alaska's first mining ventures, and effectively controlled U.S. policy for the area. On October 9, 1867, one of their employees, Benjamin Levi, hauled down the Russian flag at Sitka and was the first to raise the Stars and Stripes officially when Alaska became an American territory.

Soon after, other Jews settled in Sitka. In 1868, 14 Jews gathered together to hold a Passover *seder* using matzoh shipped from San Francisco.

The Dawson Gold Rush of 1898 attracted many Jews seeking their fortunes. When living in a tent was considered a luxury, Rosh Hashanah and Yom Kippur services were held in the Rosener store and in the Yukon Pioneer Hall. Forty people attended, chanting the prayers in Hebrew from the ample prayerbooks provided and some even wearing *tallesim*. Upon the 1902 discovery of gold in Fairbanks, many Dawson men joined that stampede, including the Jewish congregants. This group gave Fairbanks a Jewish community from the town's inception. When the town fathers set aside land for a cemetery, the Jewish community was contacted and given a plot.

However, gold fever struck again and the majority of Jews left to try their luck in Iditarod in the 1908 rush and, in 1910, the remaining group followed to Ruby. The days of the gold rushes left an important legacy; the first formally organized Jewish community in Alaska was Nome's Hebrew Benevolent Society in 1901.

As the camps played out, many moved to Anchorage which was established in 1915. Among them was Z.J. Loussac, who served as mayor of the infant community and donated the first library site.

In other areas of the state, Jews have played an important role. Sol Ripinsky opened a general store at the Haines Mission on Chilkat Peninsula in 1886. The present town of Haines grew up around the store and, now credited as the town's founder, Ripinsky is now memorialized by Mount Ripinsky in the St. Elias range.

Most of the present Jewish population of about 800 arrived after World War II. Many of them are stationed in military bases throughout the state. Many of them work for the U.S. Government or the State of Alaska. A few are employed by Alaska-based firms. A new group came in connection with the building of the trans-Alaska pipeline.

There are only two formal congregations in Alaska. Congregation Beth Sholom was founded in 1958 and follows the Reform ritual. A new temple was recently completed. The other congregation, Shomerei Ohr, is Orthodox and is in reality a shteeble. They meet in a private home located at 3427

Wentworth Street. Kosher provisions are available in the Safeway supermarket.

Anchorage

CONGREGATION BETH SHOLOM

7525 East Northern Lights   Tel. (907) 338-1836

This Reform congregation was organized in 1958. It is the northernmost congregation in the United States. Its new temple was recently completed. The congregation received assistance from the Jewish chaplain and from other Reform congregations in the "lower 48."

Fairbanks

OLDEST JEWISH BURIAL GROUND

Clay Street & 3rd Avenue

Located in the west end of the city, this is the only Jewish burial ground in Alaska. It was established in 1906 on ground donated by the city. Most Alaskan Jews who died in Alaska are returned to the "lower 48" for burial.

SYNAGOGUES

Anchorage 99504

Congregation Beth Sholom   (R)

7525 East Northern Lights   Tel. (907) 338-1836

Congregation Shomerei Ohr   (O)

3427 Wentworth Street   Tel. 278-7686

Beth Sholom in Anchorage, Alaska.

OTHER SIGHTS

Anchorage
ALASKA EXPERIENCE THEATER
705 West 6th Street   Tel. (907) 276-3730
ALASKA ZOO
O'Malley Road   Tel. (907) 344-3242
ANCHORAGE MUSEUM OF HISTORY & ART
121 West 7th Avenue   Tel. (907) 264-4326
HERITAGE LIBRARY & MUSEUM
Northern Lights Boulevard & C Street   Tel. (907) 276-1132
NOVA RIVERUNNERS OF ALASKA
Tel. (907) 745-5753
OSCAR ANDERSON HOUSE   (1915)
420 M Street   Tel. (907) 274-2336

Circle Hot Springs
ARCTIC CIRCLE HOT SPRINGS
8 miles off US 6

Cooper Landing
CHARLEY HUBBARD MINING MUSEUM
US 1
Gold panning available.

DENALI NATIONAL PARK
Tel. (907) 683-2294
NENANA RIVER FLOAT TRIPS
Tel. (907) 683-2234

Fairbanks
GOLD DREDGE #8
Goldstream Road   Tel. (907) 457-6058

NATIONAL OCEANIC ATMOSPHERIC ADMINISTRATION SATELLITE TRAKCING STATION
US 6   Tel. (907) 452-1155
Tours available.
UNIVERSITY MUSEUM
University of Alaska   Tel. (907) 474-7505

GLACIER BAY NATIONAL PARK
Tel. (907) 697-2230

Haines
CHILKAT BALD EAGLE PRESERVE FLOAT TRIPS
Tel. (907) 766-2409
FORT WILLIAM H. SEWARD
Tel. (907) 766-2540
SHELDON MUSEUM & CULTURAL CENTER
Main Street   Tel. (907) 766-2366

Homer
PRATT MUSEUM
3779 Bartlett Street   Tel. (907) 235-8635

Juneau
ALASKA STATE MUSEUM
Whittier Street   Tel. (907) 465-2901
HOUSE OF WICKERSHAM
213 7th Street   Tel. (907) 465-4563
JUNEAU DOUGLAS CITY MUSEUM
Main & 4th Streets   Tel. (907) 586-3572
MENDENHALL GLACIER
13 miles N.W. on US 7   Tel. (907) 789-0097

KATMAI NATIONAL PARK
Tel. (907) 246-3305

Kenay
FORT KENAY HISTORICAL MUSEUM
Tel. (907) 283-7294

KENAY FJORDS NATIONAL PARK
Tel. (907) 224-3175

Ketchikan
TONGASS HISTORICAL MUSEUM
629 Dock Street   Tel. (907) 225-5600
TOTEM HERITAGE CENTER
601 Deermont Street   Tel. (907) 225-5900

Kodiak
BARANOV MUSEUM
Erskine House on the harbor front , Tel. (907) 486-5920

LAKE CLARK NATIONAL PARK

MISTY FJORDS NATIONAL MONUMENT
Tel. (907) 225-2148

Nome
CARRIE McLAIN MEMORIAL MUSEUM
Front Street   Tel. (907) 443-5133

Palmer
MUSEUM OF ALASKA TRANSPORTATION & INDUSTRY
Milepost 40.2 on Glenn Highway   Tel. (907) 745-4493

Petersburg
CLAUSEN MEMORIAL MUSEUM
Fram & 2nd Streets   Tel. (907) 772-3598

Sitka
ISABELLE MILLER MUSEUM
Centennial Building   Tel. (907) 747-6455
SHELDON JACKSON MUSEUM
104 College Drive

Skagway
KLONDIKE GOLD RUSH NATIONAL HISTORICAL PARK
Tel. (907) 983-2921
TRAIL OF '98 MUSEUM
7th Avenue & Spring Street   Tel. (907) 983-2420

Valdez
PIPELINE TERMINAL TOUR (Gray Line)
Tel. (800) 544-2206
VALDEZ MUSEUM
Egan & Chenega Drives   Tel. (907) 835-2764
WORTHINGTON GLACIER

Wrangell
WRANGELL MUSEUM
2nd & Bevier Streets   Tel. (907) 874-3770

ARIZONA

Discovery of gold at La Paz in 1860 attracted white settlers to Arizona including many Jews, most of whom came from California where they had been in business in gold rush mining camps. When the La Paz gold mines ran dry, many of the miners moved to Tucson. Some of the earliest Jews in Arizona include Samuel Drachman, Hyman Goldberg, William Zeckendorf (grandfather of New York's real estate entrepreneur) and Michael Goldwater (grandfather of Senator Barry Goldwater).

The first organized Jewish community is believed to have developed in the mining town of Tombstone. The first congregation, the Tombstone Hebrew Association was founded in 1861. The community dispersed in about ten years. A Jewish cemetery was dedicated in 1881.

A Jewish dance hall girl, Josephine Sarah Marcus, daughter of Henry and Sophie Marcus of San Francisco, ran away from home in 1880. She joined a troupe of dancing girls touring the Arizona Territory. She met and fell in love with Wyatt Earp, the one-time gun fighter and sheriff of Tombstone. She later married him. Wyatt Earp, who was not Jewish, is buried beside her in the Hills of Eternity Jewish cemetery near San Francisco.

Alex Levin, a Prussian Jew, married Zenona Molina, a Catholic woman from Mexico. They were among the first families to settle in Tucson. He was a brewer and in 1869 built Levin's Park, a three-acre entertainment center which included gardens, a restaurant, a theater, an opera house and other recreational facilities. Descendants of this couple include violinist Natalie (Levin) Echavarria and singer-actress Linda Ronstadt.

By the turn of the century there were about 2,000 Jews in Arizona. Impoverished Jews from the East who began coming to Phoenix for their health around 1915 substantially increased the Jewish population. The largest Jewish centers are today located in Phoenix and Tucson. There are approximately 80,000 Jews in Arizona.

Douglas

JEWISH CEMETERY

Douglas was once a prosperous town with many Jewish merchants. The Douglas Jewish cemetery was established in 1904. It measures 150 by 200 feet and is located near the Mexican border.

Phoenix

FIRST SYNAGOGUE IN PHOENIX
Temple Beth Israel (Former)
122 East Culver Street

Temple Beth Israel was founded in 1918 and was originally called the Phoenix Hebrew Center. It was the first synagogue

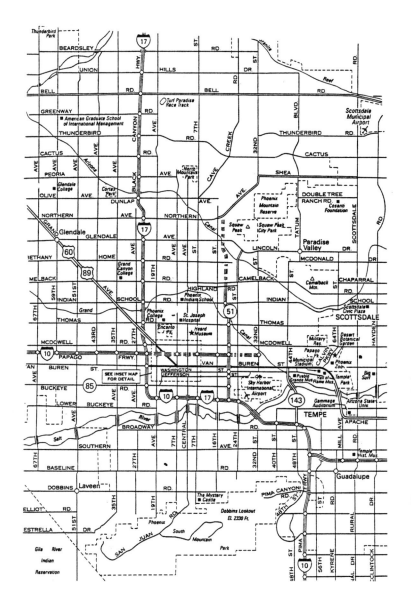

in Phoenix and was built in 1921. Dr. David Liknaitz of Los Angeles oversaw its construction and became the first rabbi of the congregation. Before the synagogue was built services were conducted over Joe Melczer's saloon. The congregation is presently located at 3310 North 10th Avenue.

The site of this former synagogue, which is presently owned by a local church, is opposite the new Deck Park, which is built over the Freeway extension.

There is another former synagogue nearby. Temple Israel's former building, built in the 1950s, is located at 3rd & McDowell. The building is presently owned by a pawn broker shop.

PLOTKIN JUDAICA MUSEUM
Temple Beth Israel
3310 North 10th Avenue   Tel. (602) 264-4428

The Plotkin Judaica Museum is housed in Temple Beth Israel. It was founded in 1967 and contains a permanent collection of Judaica, traveling exhibitions and a magnificent reproduction of a turn-of-the-century synagogue from Tunisia, complete with Moorish tile-work and silver-covered Torah cases. Museum hours are 10:00-3:00 Tuesday, Wednesday and Thursday and 12:00-3:00 on Sunday.

Be sure to see a wonderful video called "Pioneer Jews of Arizona: 1850-1920" which traces the Jewish history of the state. Copies are available in the museum.

ARIZONA BILTMORE
24th & Missouri   Tel. (602) 955-6600

The Arizona Biltmore's architectural design was inspired by the famous American architect, Frank Lloyd Wright, who worked with architect and builder, Albert Chase McArthur. For the first time in the history of architecture, precast concrete block was used as the primary interior and exterior building material of a major building. The Biltmore opened in February of 1929 and was crowned the "Jewel of the Desert."

Over the decades of its existence, the Arizona Biltmore has been a temporary home for many famous and wealthy people. President Ronald Reagan and Nancy Reagan spent their honeymoon at the Biltmore. Harpo Marx and his bride honeymooned at the Biltmore as well, and both scandalized and charmed the other guests with their lack of decorum. They were known to hold hands and skip through the formal dining room after meals. Clark Gable lost his wedding ring on the golf course, and was overjoyed when an employee found it. Spencer Tracy was known as a great tipper and made it a point of remembering the names of waitresses and bellhops.

Only a few months after the hotel opened the Stock Market crashed. The hotel was purchased by the Chicago chewing gum magnate William Wrigley, Jr. In 1973, it was sold to Talley Industries. They later engaged the Westin Hotels of Seattle to manage the Arizona Biltmore.

Today, the Arizona Biltmore is a Five-Star hotel. There are 500 guest rooms; three heated pools; 17 tennis courts, two 18-hole PGA-rated, championship golf courses, two whirlpool

Arizona Biltmore in Phoenix, designed by Frank Lloyd Wright.

spas, a Conference Center, and much more. There is a Jewish connection as well. During the week of Passover, a private caterer takes over and the Arizona Biltmore becomes glatt kosher for Passover!

Be sure to visit Frank Lloyd Wright's winter home and school of architecture, Taliesen West. It is located at 108th Street (north of East Shea Boulevard) in nearby Scottsdale. There are daily tours. For information call (602) 860-8810.

Seligman

This town located on U.S. Route 66 is named for Jesse Seligman, the New York banker and philanthropist. He financed the old Atlantic and Pacific Railroad which is now part of the Santa Fe Line. The town was founded along the railroad in 1886.

Tombstone

BOOTHILL CEMETERY

The old Boothill Cemetery of Tombstone was established in 1879. There was a Jewish section consisting of 2500 square feet. It was recently discovered by a local Indian. A new monument was built in 1984 on the site of this ancient cemetery of pioneer Jews. The monument portrays two Stars of David, a menorah and an Indian symbol.

Tucson

OLDEST SYNAGOGUE IN ARIZONA
Temple Emanu-El
520 South Stone

This synagogue was built in 1910 and was the first Jewish house of worship in the Territory of Arizona. This was two years before Arizona became a state.

JEWISH COMMUNITY CENTER
3822 East River Drive   Tel. (602) 299-7933

This newly-constructed Jewish Community Center is the hub of Jewish life in Tucson. There are programs for all age levels - from nursery to senior groups.

Yuma

ISRAELI AIR FORCE TRAINING BASES

The rugged terrain of Yuma, located at the junction of Arizona, California and Mexico, is similar to the Negev in southern Israel. The U.S. Air Force and the Israeli Air Force have a joint training program for their pilots.

KOSHER PROVISIONS

Phoenix

Karsh Bakery
  Missouri & 7th Street (Cinema Park Shopping Center)
                                    Tel. (602) 264-4874

Safeway Supermarkets

Segal's New Place (Restaurant & Market)
  4818 North 7th Street (next to Domino's Pizza)
                                    Tel. (602) 285-1515

Valley Kosher Deli
  1331 East Northern   Tel. (602) 371-0999

Tucson

Feig's Kosher Market
  5071 East 5th Street   Tel. (602) 325-2255

SYNAGOGUES

Flagstaff 86004
Heichal Ba'oranim
2609 North Patterson Boulevard   Tel. (602) 1-779-3783
Lake Havasu City
Jewish Congregation of Lake Havasu City
Tel. (602) 1-855-6833 or 1-855-3840
Mesa 85201
Temple Beth Sholom   (C)
316 South LeSeur   Tel. (602) 964-1981
Phoenix 85013
Beth Ami Temple   (R)
4545 North 36th Street   Tel. (602) 956-0805
Beth El Congregation   (C)
1118 West Glendale Avenue   Tel. (602) 944-3359
Temple Beth Israel   (R)
3310 North 10th Avenue   Tel. 264-4428
Beth Joseph Congregation   (O)
515 East Bethany Home Road   Tel. 277-8858
Chabad Lubavitch Center - Tifereth Israel (O)
2110 East Lincoln Drive   Tel. 944-2753
Temple Chai   (R)
4645 East Marilyn   Tel. 971-1234
Har Zion Congregation   (C)
5929 East Lincoln Drive   Tel. 991-0720
Temple Kol Ami   (R)
10210 North 32nd Street   Tel. 788-0939
Shaarei Tzedek Synagogue   (O)
JCC - 1718 West Maryland   Tel. 944-1133
Southwest Havurah   *Tel. 483-9303*
Temple Solel   (R)
6805 East McDonald Drive   Tel. 991-7414

Prescott 86302
Congregation B'rith Shalom   (R)
P.O.Box 2021   Tel. (602) 1-445-6758
Scottsdale 85251
Ahavat Torah Congregation   (C)
6816 East Cactus Road   Tel. (602) 991-5645
Temple Beth Emeth   (C)
6107 North Invergordon Road   Tel. 941-4112
Beth Joshua Congregation   (T)
10802 North 71st Place   Tel. 998-1565
Har Zion Congregation   (C)
5929 East Lincoln Drive   Tel. 991-0720
Scottsdale Torah Institute   (O)
14024 North 82nd Place   Tel. 443-0939
Temple Solel   (R)
6805 East McDonald Drive   Tel. 991-7414
Sierra Vista 85636
Temple Kol Hamidbar   (R)
P.O.Box 908   Tel. (602) 458-5263
Sun City 85351
Beth Emeth Congregation   (C)
13702 West Meeker Boulevard   Tel. (602) 584-7210
Temple Beth Shalom   (R)
12202 - 101st Avenue   Tel. 977-3240
Sun Lakes 85248
Sun Lakes Jewish Congregation
P.O.Box 122   Tel. (602) 1-895-8605
Tempe 85283
Temple Emanu-El   (R)
5801 South Rural Road   Tel. (602) 838-1414
Hillel Union of Jewish Studies
1012 South Mill Avenue   Tel. 967-7563
Tucson 85711
Congregation Anshei Israel   (C)
5550 East 5th Street   Tel. (602) 745-5550

Beth Shalom Congregation   (C)
                          2915 Indian Rains Road   Tel. 296-2735
Chabad House   (O)   *1301 East Elm Street   Tel. 881-7955*
Congregation Chaverim   (R)
                          2777 North Santa Marta Place   Tel. 885-2855
Congregation Chofetz Chaim   (O)
                          5150 East 5th Street   Tel. 747-7780
Temple Emanu-El   (R)
                          225 North Country Club   Tel. 327-4501
Young Israel   (O)   *2443 East 4th Street   Tel. 326-8362*
Yuma
Congregation Beth Hamidbar   *Tel. (602) 1-726-9650*

MIKVEHS

Phoenix
Congregation Beth Joseph
          515 East Bethany Home Road   Tel. (602) 277-8858
Tucson
Mikveh of Tucson   (Young Israel)
          2443 East 4th Street   Tel. (602) 745-0958 or 326-7739

OTHER SIGHTS

Apache Junction
GOLDFIELD GHOST TOWN & MINE TOURS
3 miles north on US 88   Tel. (602) 983-0333

Bisbee
BISBEE HISTORICAL SOCIETY MUSEUM
37 Main Street   Tel. (602) 432-2141
BISBEE MINING & HISTORICAL MUSEUM
5 Copper Queen Plaza   Tel. (602) 432-7071
THE LAVENDER PIT (Copper Mine Tours)
Tel. (602) 432-2071
MUHEIM HERITAGE HOUSE
207 Youngblood Hill
QUEEN MINE TOURS
Tel. (602) 432-2071

Camp Verde
YAVAPAI-APACHE VISITOR CENTER
Middle Verde exit on I-17   Tel. (602) 567-5276

CANYON DE CHELLY NATIONAL MONUMENT
Tel. (602) 674-5436

Casa Grande
CASA GRANDE VALLEY HISTORICAL MUSEUM
110 West Florence Road   Tel. (602) 836-2223
CASA GRANDE RUINS NATIONAL MONUMENT
Tel. (602) 723-3172

CHIRICAHUA NATIONAL MONUMENT
70 mile N.E. of Douglas via US 666 and Route 181

Cordes Junction
ARCOSANTI
2 miles east of I-17
Architect Paolo Soleri's city of the future.   Tel. (602) 632-7135

Douglas
GLADSTONE HOTEL   (1906)
1046 G Avenue

Dragoon
AMERIND FOUNDATION MUSEUM
Tel. (602) 586-3666

Flagstaff
LOWELL OBSERVATORY
Santa Fe Avenue & Mars Hill   Tel. (602) 774-2096
MUSEUM OF NORTHERN ARIZONA
Fort Valley Road   Tel. (602) 774-5211

Florence
PINAL COUNTY HISTORICAL MUSEUM
715 South Main Street   Tel. (602) 868-4382

Ganado
**HUBBELL TRADING POST NATIONAL HISTORIC
SITE (1878)**
US 264   Tel. (602) 755-3475

Gila Bend
PAINTED ROCKS STATE PARK

Globe
SALT RIVER RAFT TRIPS
Tel. (915) 371-2489

GRAND CANYON CAVERNS

Route 66   Tel. (602) 422-3223

GRAND CANYON NATIONAL PARK

The canyon is 277 miles long and averages 10 miles in width from rim to rim; it is 5,700 feet deep at the North Rim.

Tel. (602) 638-2245

GRAND CANYON TRAIL GUIDES   Tel. (602) 638-2391

HORSEBACK RIDES   Tel. (602) 638-2424

YAVAPAI MUSEUM

East Rim of Grand Canyon

HOOVER DAM

LAKE MEADE NATIONAL RECREATIONAL AREA

Lake Meade was created when the Hoover Dam was built in 1936. It is one of the largest manmade lakes in the Western Hemisphere. Hoover Dam is 726 feet high. There are tours down in the powerplant. There is an Exhibit Building with a 15-minute talk.

Kingman

MOHAVE MUSEUM OF HISTORY & ART

400 West Beale Street   Tel. (602) 753-3195

Lake Havasu City

LONDON BRIDGE

Robert P. McCulloch purchased the London Bridge and had it transported block by block from England in 1971.

Mesa

ARIZONA MUSEUM FOR YOUTH

35 North Robson Street   Tel. (602) 644-2467

ROCKIN' R RANCH

6136 East Baseline Road   Tel. (602) 832-1539

CHAMPLIN FIGHTER MUSEUM

4636 Fighter Aces Drive at Falcon Field   Tel. (602) 830-4540

MESA SOUTHWEST MUSEUM
53 North MacDonald Street   Tel. (602) 834-2230

MONTEZUMA CASTLE NATIONAL MONUMENT
Prehistoric cliff dwellings from the 12th century.
Tel. (602) 567-3322

MONUMENT VALLEY NAVAJO TRIBAL PARK
MYSTERY VALLEY
Isolated monoliths of red sandstone tower as much as 1,000 feet
above the valley floor.   Tel. (602) 727-3287

Nogales
PIMERIA ALTA HISTORICAL SOCIETY MUSEUM
223 Grand Avenue   Tel. (602) 287-5402

Page
JOHN WESLEY POWELL MUSEUM
Lake Powell Boulevard & Navajo Drive   Tel. (602) 645-9496

Parker
COLORADO RIVER INDIAN TRIBES MUSEUM
2nd & Mohave Streets   Tel. (602) 669-9211

Patagonia
STRADLING MUSEUM OF THE HORSE
Route 82   Tel. (602) 394-2264

Payson
TONTO NATURAL BRIDGE
11 miles north on Route 87   Tel. (602) 476-3440
ZANE GREY'S CABIN
Tel. (602) 478-4243

PETRIFIED FOREST NATIONAL PARK
US 180   Tel. (602) 524-6228

This area was once a great swamp with huge trees. The dead logs were buried in sediments rich in volcanic ash. Slowly silica impregnated the logs until they became virtually solid stone. Iron oxide and other minerals stained the silica to produce rainbow colors. Don't expect to find any live trees or swamps today. There are just mounds of fragments of multi-colored tree trunks scattered over many hundreds of acres.

Phoenix
ARIZONA STATE CAPITOL MUSEUM
Washington Street & 17th Avenue   Tel. (602) 542-4581
DESERT BOTANICAL GARDEN
1201 North Galvin Parkway   Tel. (602) 941-1217
HALL OF FLAME MUSEUM
6101 East Van Buren Street   Tel. (602) 275-3473
HEARD MUSEUM (American Indian)
22 East Monte Vista Road   Tel. (602) 252-8848
HERITAGE SQUARE
6th & Monros Streets
MYSTERY CASTLE
800 East Mineral Road (South Mountain Park) Tel. 268-1581
PHOENIX ART MUSEUM
1625 North Central Avenue   Tel. (602) 257-1222
PIONEER ARIZONA LIVING HISTORY MUSEUM
I-17 to Pioneer Road exit   Tel. (602) 993-0212
PUEBLO GRANDE MUSEUM
4619 East Washington Street   Tel. (602) 275-3452

Prescott
PHIPPEN MUSEUM
4701 US 89 North   Tel. (602) 778-1385
SHARLOT HALL MUSEUM
415 West Gurley Street   Tel. (602) 445-3122

SMOKI MUSEUM
Arizona Avenue   Tel. (602) 445-1230

Sacaton
GILA INDIAN CENTER
I-10 (exit 175)   Tel. (602) 963-2981

SAGUARO NATIONAL MONUMENT
The saguaro cactus grows only in southern Arizona.

St. Johns
APACHE COUNTY MUSEUM
180 West Cleveland Street   Tel. (602) 337-4737

Scottsdale
COSANTI FOUNDATION
6433 Doubletree Road   Tel. (602) 948-6145
Headquarters and workshop of architect Paolo Soleri.
RAWHIDE
23023 Scottsdale Road   Tel. (602) 563-5111
TALIESIN WEST
108th Street, near East Shea Boulevard   Tel. (602) 860-8810
Winter home and architectural school of Frank Lloyd Wright. Tours
are given hourly.

Sedona
RED ROCKS OF SEDONA
US 89A   (must see)
SEDONA ARTS CENTER
Tel. (602) 282-3809

Superior
BOYCE THOMPSON SOUTHWESTERN ARBORETUM
3 miles west on US 60   Tel. (602) 689-2811

Tempe

GAMMAGE CENTER FOR THE PERFORMING ARTS

Arizona State University

One of the last major buildings designed by Frank Lloyd Wright.

ARIZONA STATE UNIVERSITY FINE ARTS CENTER

10th Street & Mill Avenue   Tel. (602) 965-ARTS

MUSEUM OF GEOLOGY

University Drive & McAllister Street   Tel. (602) 965-5768

TEMPLE HISTORICAL MUSEUM

Rural Road & Southern Avenue   Tel. (602) 731-8842

Thatcher

MUSEUM OF ANTHROPOLOGY

Eastern Arizona College   Tel. (602) 428-1133

Tombstone

BIRD CAGE THEATRE

6th & Allen Streets

CAMILLUS FLY STUDIO

Fremont & 3rd Streets

HISTORAMA

 Tel. (602) 457-3456

O.K.CORRAL

Allen & 4th Streets   Tel. (602) 457-3456

ROSS TREE INN MUSEUM

4th & Toughnut Streets   Tel. (602) 457-3326

SCHIEFFELIN HALL

4th & Fremont Streets

SILVER NUGGET MUSEUM

Allen & 6th Streets   Tel. (602) 457-3310

TOMBSTONE COURTHOUSE

219 East Toughnut Street   Tel. (602) 457-3311

Tucson

ARIZONA-SONORA DESERT MUSEUM
Tucson Mountain Park   Tel. (602) 883-1380
ARIZONA STATE MUSEUM
Park Avenue   (University of Arizona)   Tel. (602) 621-6302
COLOSSAL CAVE
Tel. (602) 791-7677
DE GRAZIA GALLERY IN THE SUN
6300 North Swan Road   Tel. (602) 299-9191
FORT LOWELL MUSEUM
Craycroft & Fort Lowell Roads   Tel. (602) 885-3832
GRACE H. FLANDRAU PLANETARIUM
University Boulevard & Cherry Avenue   Tel. (602) 621-4515
JOHN C. FREMONT HOUSE   (1858)
151 South Granada Avenue   Tel. (602) 622-0956

KITT PEAK NATIONAL OBSERVATORY
56 miles S.W. off US 86   Tel. (602) 620-5350
MINERAL MUSEUM
North Drive (Geology Building)   Tel. (602) 621-4227
OLD TUCSON
Speedway Boulevard   Tel. (602) 883-0100
PIMA AIR MUSEUM
6000 East Valencia Road   Tel. (602) 574-9658
TUCSON MOUNTAIN PARK
8 miles west on Speedway Boulevard & Kinney Road
TUCSON MUSEUM
949 East 2nd Street   Tel. (602) 628-5774
TUCSON MUSEUM OF ART
140 North Main Street   Tel. (602) 624-2333
UNIVERSITY OF ARIZONA MUSEUM OF ART
Olive Avenue & Speedway Boulevard   Tel. (602) 621-7567

WALNUT CANYON NATIONAL MONUMENT
Cliff dwellings inhabited by the Sinagua Indians about 1120-1250.
Tel. (602) 526-3367

Wickenburg
DESERT CABALLEROS WESTERN MUSEUM
20 North Frontier Street   Tel. (602) 684-2272

Willcox
COCHISE MUSEUM
Near junction I-10 & US 186   Tel. (602) 384-2272

Williams
GRAND CANYON DEER FARM
100 Deer Farm Road   Tel. (602) 635-2357

Window Rock
NAVAJO TRIBAL MUSEUM
US 264   Tel. (602) 871-6673

Winslow
METEOR CRATER
19 miles west and 6 miles south of I-40. Diameter of the rim is
4,150 feet and is 570 feet deep.   Tel. (602) 774-8350

Yuma
ARIZONA CENTURY HOUSE MUSEUM & GARDENS
240 Madison Avenue   Tel. (602) 782-1841
FORT YUMA QUECHAN MUSEUM
Fort Yuma Indian Hill   Tel. (602) 572-0661
YUMA ART CENTER
281 Gila Street   Tel. (602) 783-2314
YUMA TERRITORIAL PRISON   (1876)
4th Street

CALIFORNIA

Gold was discovered at Sutter's mill near Sacramento in January, 1848. This was the beginning of the Gold Rush. Hundreds of Jews were among the 3,000,000 gold miners who traveled from all parts of the world to seek their fortunes. Many of the first Jewish settlers were peddlers who later expanded into stores in a number of towns and mining camps. They were involved with clothing, dry goods, tobacco, cattle, stationery, food and mining supplies.

Many Jews settled in the large towns such as San Francisco, Los Angeles, Sacramento, San Diego and San Jose, which was California's first state capital. Others established congregations and burial societies in their own mining camps and towns such as Jackson, Grass Valley, San Andreas, Sonora, Mariposa, Coloma, Nevada City, Shasta and Folsom.

There were at least 1,000 Jews in Mining Camp Towns during the Gold Rush, between 1849 and 1888, but almost every year there was a different 1,000. A few stayed on and continued to do business in the mining towns but most who failed to strike it rich either in the mines or in business moved elsewhere. When the ore in the mines began to be worked out by the end of the 1870s, the miners left and the towns they had established deteriorated, and in some cases became ghost towns. Six of the old Jewish cemeteries from the Gold Rush era have recently been restored.

The first Jews arrived in Los Angeles in the 1850s. The first synagogue established in 1862 was today's Wilshire Boulevard Temple. The first settlers lived near today's downtown section.

Around the turn of the century, the Jewish population increased dramatically when several thousand Jews from the East Coast cities of New York, Philadelphia and Baltimore who contracted tuberculosis in the sweatshops of the clothing industry were advised to move to the warmer climates of California. Another increase in the Jewish population occurred following the devastating Great Earthquake and Fire of 1906 in San Francisco.

The founding fathers of the movie industry were almost all Jews. Many were originally clothiers, garment workers, junk dealers, nickelodeon operators and furriers. Some of the notable Jewish movie producers include Adolph Zukor, Jesse Lasky, Carl Laemmle, William Fox, Lewis Selnick, Samuel Goldwyn, the Warner Brothers, the Cohn Brothers, and Louis B. Mayer. They created such motion picture companies as Columbia Pictures, Universal, Paramount and Metro-Goldwyn-Meyer (MGM).

The first motion picture, *The Squaw Man*, was produced by Jesse Lasky, Samuel Goldwyn and Cecil B. DeMill. The Warner Brothers started with the Vitagraph Studios in Brooklyn (site of today's Shulamith Girl's Yeshiva in Flatbush). They produced the first "talkie" on the West Coast, *The Jazz Singer*, starring Al Jolson.

Today, most of California's film industry is controlled by conglomerates, but Jews are still heavily represented in the ranks of film writers, producers, directors, agents, technicians, musicians and actors.

The first major Jewish neighborhood in Los Angeles was in the Boyle Heights section. During the 1940s and 1950s the

Jews moved to the Fairfax Avenue area. That section is now called the Lower East Side of Los Angeles. There are scores of kosher restaurants, Judaica shops, synagogues and yeshivas. Another major Jewish area is the nearby Pico-Robertston section.

There are approximately 800,000 Jews living in the greater Los Angeles area. It is the second largest Jewish population in the country. There are about 50,000 Israelis and some 30,000 Iranian Jews in Los Angeles. There are approximately 95,000 Jews in the San Francisco Bay area.

Berkeley

JUDAH L. MAGNES MEMORIAL MUSEUM
2911 Russell Street (94705) Tel. 849-2710

This museum is named in honor of Dr. Judah L. Magnes who was the first native Californian to be ordained a rabbi, and later served both Reform and Conservative congregations in New York. The museum was founded in 1962 by Seymour Fromer and is housed in a four-story mansion.

The museum contains the Goldstein Library of Judaica, Holocaust Room, Archaeology Room, Textile Room, Festival Room and the Western Jewish History Center.

Museum hours: Mon - Fri   12 - 4 p.m. Note: The museum is located near Claremont Avenue.

Colma

WYATT EARP'S GRAVE
Hills of Eternity Cemetery

The last resting place of the legendary Marshall Wyatt Earp is in the section owned by San Francisco's Congregation Sherith Israel. Wyatt Earp was not a Jew, but he was married to the Jewish dance hall girl, Josephine Marcus of San Francisco. When the famous sheriff of Dodge City died in 1929, she insisted that he be buried in her family plot. The small black granite gravestone is located in the back of section D-2.

How to get there: From San Francisco, take Freeway 280 south to Route 82. Continue south for about a mile. The cemetery is on the left side of the road.

Wyatt Earp's grave near San Francisco.

Los Angeles

FIRST JEWISH SITE - STATE HISTORICAL MARKER
Lilac Terrace & Lookout Drive

The State Historical Marker at the location of the first Jewish cemetery in Los Angeles also commemorates Los Angeles' first Jewish institution. The Hebrew Benevolent Society was organized on July 2, 1854 for the purpose of "procuring a piece of land for the burying ground." It was the first charitable organization in the city.

The site, on Lilac Terrace and Lookout Drive (Chavez Ravine), near Dodger Stadium, is now a Naval Armory, but during its service as a cemetery was adjacent to the Jewish neighborhoods downtown, on Bunker Hill and around Temple Street. When the location was no longer suitable for a cemetery in 1910, due to oil drilling on surrounding property, the remains and monuments were transferred to Home of Peace cemetery.

How to get there: Take the Pasadena Freeway to Stadium Way; turn left on stadium to Lookout Drive; go up Lookout to Lilac Terrace; turn left on Lilac - the Historic Marker is about 300 feet ahead.

FIRST SYNAGOGUE IN LOS ANGELES
Wilshire Boulevard Temple
3663 Wilshire Boulevard   Tel. (213) 388-2401

Jews first settled in Los Angeles in the late 1840s. In 1862 the Temple was chartered as Congregation B'nai Brith and in

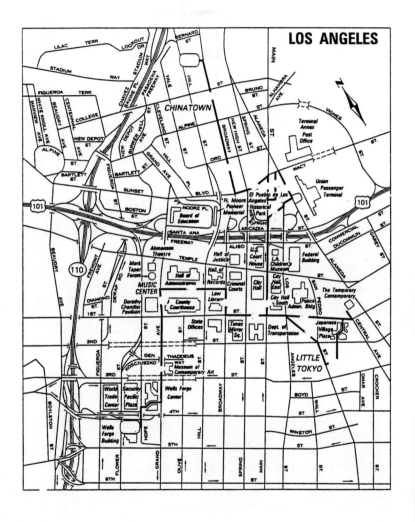

First synagogue in Los Angeles was built in 1873.

B'nai B'rith's second location, 9th & Hope Streets, in 1896.

Warner Murals in the Wilshire Boulevard Temple.

1872 the congregation dedicated its first synagogue on Fort Street (now Broadway). A small plaque on the sidewalk near 214 South Broadway commemorates the site of the first synagogue in Los Angeles.

As Los Angeles grew so did the congregation, and in 1895 they moved to a larger structure at Ninth and Hope Streets. The move to the present location and the change in name to Wilshire Boulevard Temple happened in 1929. This outstanding religious structure is a Los Angeles historical landmark and is listed in the United States Register of Historic Places.

The Edgar F. Magnin Sanctuary, named after the congregation's noted rabbi, is a magnificent house of worship, from its splendid stained glass windows to its circular dome rising 125 feet overhead. The impressive Warner Murals designed by Hugo Ballin bring 3,000 years of Jewish history and beauty to worshipers as well as visitors from around the world. Be sure to visit the Maxwell H. Dubin and Alfred Wolf Exhibit Center with its treasures of Judaica from around the world. The Wilshire Boulevard Temple follows the Reform ritual and has a family membership of approximately 2,450.

THE OLD NEIGHBORHOOD - BOYLE HEIGHTS

During the 1920s a major Jewish migration crossed to the East banks of the Los Angeles River to Boyle Heights. By 1930, the Jewish population in the "Heights" numbered some 10,000 families. The Heights were known as the "Lower East Side" of Los Angeles. There were scores of synagogues, yeshivas, kosher butchers, groceries, delis and bakeries. The main street and shopping area was along Brooklyn Avenue.

Today, this section is part of East Los Angeles' barrio. All that remains of this once thriving Jewish neighborhood is the old Breed Street Shul.

BREED STREET SHUL
Congregation Talmud Torah
247 North Breed Street

This is one of the oldest Orthodox synagogues in Los Angeles. It is the last surviving synagogue in the Boyle Heights section. Services are now held only on the Sabbath and on holidays. The Breed Street Shul is a major Los Angeles landmark. It was featured in both the 1927 and 1980 versions of the movie *The Jazz Singer*. The 1927 film featured the Jewish actor and singer Al Jolson. It was the first "talkie," talking motion picture and also featured the sound track of cantor Yossele Rosenblatt.

HEBREW SHELTERING SOCIETY (FORMER)
131 South Boyle Avenue

The Hebrew Sheltering Society was founded in 1911 as a temporary facility for the homeless, transient and down- and-out but soon became a haven for the aged as well. It later moved to Boyle and Fourth and was known as the Los Angeles Jewish Home for the Aging. In the 1970s the Home relocated to the San Fernando Valley. The Boyle Heights facility now serves as a home for the aged for the Japanese community.

SOTO-MICHIGAN CENTER
Soto & Michigan Streets

This building was built in 1927 for the Jewish Centers Association of Los Angeles. As the Jews began to leave Boyle Heights, the center was renamed the Eastside Center. Closing its doors in 1957, the building has been turned into a Chicano community center.

KASPARE COHN HOSPITAL (FORMER)
1443 Carrol Avenue

Kaspare Cohn, founder of today's Union Bank and one of Los Angeles' wealthiest citizens, donated this house as a hospital for Jewish tuberculosis patients in 1902. This was at the time of peak Jewish immigration. Many immigrants were indigent tuberculosis victims escaping the sweatshops of New York City, Boston, Baltimore and Philadelphia for Los Angeles' healthier climate.

Many of the hospital's neighbors complained that land values would fall in this once-fashionable area. The hospital was forced to move beyond the city limits, to Whittier Boulevard in East Los Angeles. This institution became a general medical facility, the Cedars of Lebanon Hospital. It evolved into today's Cedars-Sinai Medical Center.

HOME OF PEACE CEMETERY
4334 Whittier Boulevard   Tel. (213) 388-3161

This cemetery is owned and operated by the Wilshire Boulevard Temple. It is the site to which the graves from the original Hebrew Benevolent Society cemetery were transferred. It is located just east of Boyle Heights.

The resting place of Los Angeles' original Jewish settlers can still be seen along with those of Warner Brothers; Fanny Brice; Los Angeles' first and only police chief, Emil Harris; and a Jewish Civil War veteran.

Tours can be arranged by calling the cemetery office.

Driving Tour - Homes of Jewish Movie Stars

Note: Some of these homes have been sold over the years to other personalities.

Morey Amsterdam   *1012 Hillcrest Drive*   (Beverly Hills)

Jack Benny   *1002 Roxbury Drive*   (Beverly Hills)

Milton Berle   *908 Crescent Drive*   (Beverly Hills)

Fanny Brice   *312 North Faring Road*   (Beverly Hills)

George Burns and Gracie Allen   *720 Maple Drive*   (B.H.)
                                16050 Valley Vista   (Encino)

Red Buttons   *778 Tortuoso Way*   (Bel Air)

Eddie Cantor   *9360 Monte Leon Lane*   (Beverly Hills)

Jack Carter   *603 Foothill Road*   (Beverly Hills)

Charlie Chaplin   *1085 Summit Drive*   (Beverly Hills)

Sammy Davis Jr.   *1151 Summit Drive*   (Beverly Hills)

Eddie Fisher   *1328 Beverly Estate Drive*   (Beverly Hills)

Samuel Goldwyn   *1200 Laurel Lane*   (Beverly Hills)

Lorne Greene   *2090 Mandeville Canyon*   (Los Angeles)

Buddy Hackett   *718 Walden Drive*   (Beverly Hills)

George Jessel   *972 Ocean Front Drive*   (Los Angeles)

Al Jolson   *4875 Louise Avenue*   (Encino)

Danny Kaye   *1103 San Ysidro Drive*   (Bel Air)

Oscar Levant   *905 Roxbury Drive*   (Beverly Hills)

Jerry Lewis   *322 St. Cloud Road*   (Bel Air)

Louis B. Mayer   *322 St. Cloud Road*   (Bel Air)

Carl Reiner   *714 Rodeo Drive*   (Beverly Hills)

Don Rickles   *10433 Wilshire Boulevard*   (Los Angeles)

Barbara Streisand   *301 Carolwood Drive*   (Bel Air)

Note: Be sure to visit Beverly Hills, Bel Air, Westwood, and Brentwood on Sunday afternoons. Some of the multi-million-dollar mansions which are for sale are "open-to-the-public" from 1:00-4:00 p.m. Look for the little flags and the "open house" signs along the roads. There is no obligation to buy, but it's very exciting just to see some of these homes.

HILLCREST COUNTRY CLUB
West Pico Boulevard & Avenue of the Stars

The Los Angeles Country Club is still a "restricted" club - no Jews are allowed to be members! In order to combat this blatantly anti-Semitic act, the Jewish community organized its own private club, the Hillcrest Country Club, located just a few blocks south of the L.A. Country Club. This club does not discriminate but one of the provisions for joining is that all members must donate a large sum of money to Jewish charities.

It pays to belong to the Hillcrest Country Club, since a large proportion of the personalities in the movie, television and music industry in Hollywood are Jewish and belong to this club.

SYNAGOGUE FOR THE PERFORMING ARTS

1727 Barrington Court, Suite 205   Tel. (213) 472-3500

All members of this unique congregation have a direct connection with the entertainment "industry." Call for schedule of services.

SINAI TEMPLE

10400 Wilshire Boulevard   Tel. (213) 474-1518

This is the oldest Conservative congregation in the city. It was organized in 1906. Its first synagogue building was located at 12th and Valencia. It is now used by a Welsh Presbyterian church. Its second and more ornate structure was located at 4th and New Hampshire. It was built in 1925, still has its original Hebrew cornerstone but has been purchased by a local Korean church.

Sinai Temple is presently located at Wilshire Boulevard and Beverly Glen. It was dedicated in 1961 and designed by the noted architect, Sidney Eisenshtat. In 1981, the Kraus Pavilion and the Don Rickles gymnasium were completed.

SKIRBALL MUSEUM
Hebrew Union College

3077 University Mall   (90007)   Tel. (213) 749-3424

The Skirball Museum is located in downtown Los Angeles near the University of Southern California. The museum houses one of the world's outstanding collections of Judaica and provides a two-fold history of the Jewish people through ceremonial art and archaeological artifacts.

The Skirball Museum will be moving in 1992 to its new location in Bel Air, at Mulholland Drive and the west side of Route 405 (San Diego Freeway). The new museum and cultural center will be designed by the noted architect, Moshe Safdie.

Museum hours: Tuesday - Friday 11-4   Sunday 10-5.

STEPHEN S. WISE TEMPLE
15500 Stephen S. Wise Drive   Tel. (213) 476-8561

As you drive up the main entrance to this hillside temple and Hebrew school complex be prepared to undergo a security check (by Israeli guards). The terraced site is one of the most exciting locations in Los Angeles. Since there is a large pool within the complex, some people call it the "shul with the pool." The temple is located in the exclusive Bel Air section. The congregation follows the Reform ritual and has a family membership of approximately 2,750.

MUSEUM OF THE HOLOCAUST &
MARTYRS MEMORIAL
6505 Wilshire Boulevard   (90048)   Tel. (213) 852-1234

Located on the ground floor of the Jewish Community Building, the Museum of the Holocaust is at once a memorial, museum, chapel and library. The Memorial is affiliated with Yad VaShem, the official Israeli Holocaust study center in Jerusalem. Tours are available and are often led by Holocaust survivors.

SIMON WIESENTHAL CENTER
Beit Hashoah-Museum of Tolerance
9760 West Pico Boulevard   (90035)   Tel. (213) 553-9306

The Wiesenthal Center is dedicated to studying, interpreting and educating the public about the events of the Holocaust. There is a Museum of the Holocaust, a specially prepared multi-media presentation on World War II. The Wiesenthal Center is housed on the campus of Yeshiva University in Los Angeles (YULA).

The new Beit Hashoah - Museum of Tolerance was designed by the firm of Starkman, Vidal & Christenson.

OLDEST SEPHARDIC CONGREGATION
Sephardic Hebrew Center
4911 West 59th Street   (90034)   Tel. (213) 295-5541

Los Angeles' oldest Sephardic congregation was founded in 1917 by a group of young Sephardic men from the island of Rhodes. Originally named Peace and Progress Society, the synagogue built its first building at 55th and Hoover Streets in 1935. That building now houses an African Methodist Episcopal church. The congregation moved to its present location in 1966.

SEPHARDIC TEMPLE TIFERETH ISRAEL
10500 Wilshire Boulevard   Tel. (213) 475-7311

Members of this congregation originate from such Sephardic countries as Turkey, Greece, the Balkans, North Africa and Cuba. The temple features an outdoor Spanish garden, a

Sephardic library and a museum. The exterior of the temple was designed in white precast concrete blocks and was intended to simulate Jerusalem stone. The congregation follows the Conservative Sephardic ritual.

UNIVERSITY OF JUDAISM
15600 Mulholland Drive   Tel. (213) 476-9777

The University of Judaism is the West Coast affiliate of the Conservative movement's Jewish Theological Seminary of America. The campus is located on top of a mountain in Bel Air and offers extraordinary views of the San Fernando Valley. There are occasional exhibitions on display in the University's gallery space.

CHABAD WEST COAST HEADQUARTERS
741 Gayley Avenue (Westwood) Tel. (213) 208-7511

Chabad Houses are branches of the Lubavitch Chassidic Movement whose world headquarters are located at 770 Eastern Parkway, Brooklyn, New York. Each Chabad House has an outreach program which assists Jews of all backgrounds and ages; college students, newly-arrived Russian immigrants, people in need of drug rehabilitation, etc.

This Chabad House, located next to the UCLA campus in Westwood Village, had a catastrophic tragedy several years ago. A fire completely destroyed the building and the Torahs. Three people perished in the blaze. An urgent appeal went out throughout the Los Angeles Jewish community. Many personalities in the entertainment industry put together a

Chabad West Coast Headquarters.

telethon which raised several million dollars to help rebuild.

The Chabad House was recently rebuilt in a very unique design. It was designed in English Tudor, as an exact replica of the World Headquarters of the Lubavitch Movement located at 770 Eastern Parkway, in Brooklyn, New York!

BETH JACOB CONGREGATION
1490 South Robertson Boulevard   Tel. (213) 275-5640

This is the largest Orthodox congregation "west of Lincoln Square Synagogue" in New York City. The main sanctuary just cannot accommodate all who wish to attend. There is standing room only for late-comers. The "upstairs minyan" has relocated to a nearby Hebrew academy. The synagogue is located in the Pico-Robertson section.

Note: There is an Eruv in the western portion of Los Angeles. The boundaries are from La Cienega Boulevard to Route 405 and from West Pico Boulevard to Sunset Boulevard. For further information, call the Eruv "hot line" at (213) 275-ERUV.

FAIRFAX COMMUNITY MURAL
South Wall of People's Market Building
North Fairfax & Oakwood Avenues

The Fairfax Community Mural design features a sequence of seven chronological panels depicting Jewish life in Los Angeles from the 1840s to the present day. The images were painted directly from 35 authentic historical photographs.

The mural was conceived as an intergenerational community service project involving senior citizens and teens, both Jewish and non-Jewish, from the Fairfax area. These volunteers worked together with a team of professional artists and historians and created this 21 foot by 111 foot mural. It was dedicated on September 8, 1985.

Some of the scenes in the mural depict the oldest synagogue in Los Angeles, the filming of Jesse Lasky's 1913 silent movie, Al Jolson in *The Jazz Singer*, the Support-for-Israel rally in the Hollywood Bowl and Sandy Koufax pitching a 1964 no-hitter.

Note: Canter's Deli is not kosher but kosher-style.

Fairfax Communal Mural.

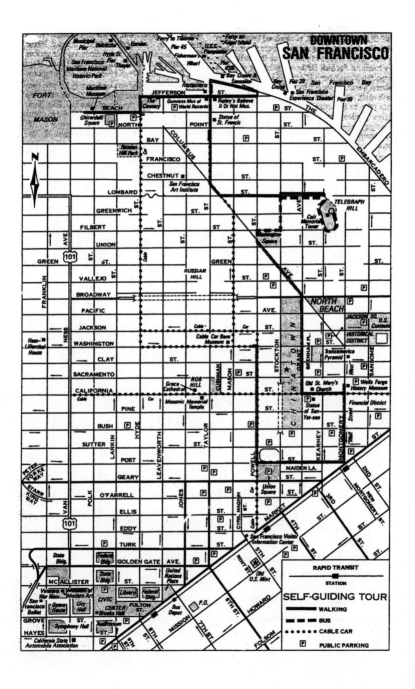

San Francisco

FIRST GOLD RUSH SYNAGOGUE SERVICES
Montgomery & Washington Streets

The site of the first religious services during the Gold Rush is marked by a plaque on the eastern façade of the "old" Trans-America Building, located just across the street from the new "pyramid" Trans-America Building, at Montgomery and Washington Streets. Forty Jewish pioneers gathered to conduct the first known Jewish worship service in California on September 26, 1849 on the second floor of a store at that site.

ONLY SYNAGOGUE TO SURVIVE GREAT QUAKE
Temple Sherith Israel
2266 California Street   Tel. (415) 346-1720

This congregation was organized on August 20, 1850. Its first synagogue was built in 1854 and was located on Stockton Street, between Broadway and Vallejo Street. In 1870, a second building was constructed at Post and Taylor Streets. On February 22, 1904, the cornerstone of the present temple was officially laid.

Sherith Israel withstood San Francisco's most famous disaster - the Great Earthquake and Fire of 1906. The building was located in the new area of the "Western Addition." The fire was blocked at Van Ness Avenue when all of the buildings along that street were ordered blown up to create a fire-break.

Sherith Israel was one of the few public structures remaining in the smoking ruins of the city.

The city's Superior Courts met in Sherith Israel for more than two years. Here were held the famous trials of corrupt city officials. In 1945, a founding session of the United Nations was held in the Main Sanctuary of Temple Sherith Israel. The congregation follows the Reform ritual.

Sherith Israel survived San Francisco's earthquake of 1906.

HASS-LILIENTHAL HOUSE
2007 Franklin Street   Tel. (415) 441-3000

William Hass, a Bavarian Jew who immigrated to San Francisco in the 1860s, started out in the wholesale grocery business. He then expanded his ventures into mining. He built this house in the Pacific Heights section in 1886. This stately Victorian house was built entirely of redwood.

The Hass-Lilienthal House combines elements of two architectural styles that were popular in late Victorian San Francisco at the end of the 19th century. The rectangular bays and incised ornamentation are characteristic of the San Francisco Stick style of the late 1880s. The general asymmetry of the house and many of its details - the gables, the varied shingles, the great round tower - are typical of the Queen Anne style, which dominated San Francisco residential architecture in the 1890s.

The house still has today almost all the family furnishings that were collected by the Hass and Lilienthal families through the years from 1886, when they first moved in, until 1972. The house is a designated San Francisco Landmark and is listed on the National Register of Historic Places. Tours are available on Sunday and Wednesday afternoons. The Hass-Lilienthal House's main floor and ballroom may be rented by members of the Foundation for San Francisco's Architectural Heritage which operates the house museum.

LEVI STRAUSS & COMPANY
1 Embarcadero

Hass-Lilienthal House was built in 1886.

Levi Strauss arrived in San Francisco in 1851 with a bundle of tough canvas fabric. He hoped to sell it to tentmakers and owners of covered wagons. This material was later used in the manufacturing of tough-fabric pants used by the gold miners.

JEWISH COMMUNITY MUSEUM

121 Steuart Street (94105) Tel. (415) 543-8880

The Jewish Community Museum is housed in the Jewish Federation Building. There are changing exhibitions on Jewish art, culture, history and contemporary issues with emphasis on visitor and artist involvement. Programs include performing arts, lectures, holiday celebrations and workshops.

Be sure to pick up a copy of the San Francisco Resource Guide which contains up-to-date information about synagogues, kosher restaurants, singles groups, Israeli folk dancing, and much more throughout the San Francisco Bay area.

THE OLD JEWISH NEIGHBORHOOD

Around the turn of the century, there was a large Jewish neighborhood near today's downtown section. After the Great Earthquake and Fire of 1906 the community shifted around Fillmore Street. All that remains of the Jewish presence is the old Mount Zion Hospital and the former Ohabei Sholame synagogue. That Moorish Revival building, located in the heart of today's Little Japan, on Bush Street (east of Laguna), is used by a local Japanese club. It has been declared an historic landmark. Another prominent congregation in that section was Keneseth Israel. It is still functioning in a downtown location,

655 Sutter Street (suite 203).

SUTRO HEIGHTS
Temescal Street

Adolph Sutro was a mining engineer, philanthropist and pioneer builder in San Francisco. He was born in Prussia and came to San Francisco in 1851. He built Sutro Heights which he presented to the city as a public park. Sutro built his Cliff House in the 1880s opposite the Heights. It was destroyed by fire in 1907. The present Cliff House was built in 1907 and is a landmark restaurant. Be sure to visit the old-fashioned penny-arcade with original antique games on the lower level of the Cliff House. Note: You can view the seals on Seal Rocks located just west of the Cliff House. If you wish to view sea lions go to Pier 39 at Fisherman's Wharf.

As an engineer, Adolph Sutro designed the Sutro drainage and ventilating tunnel for the Comstock Lode in Virginia City, Nevada. Adolph Sutro was mayor of San Francisco from 1895-96. Sutro Heights is now part of the University of San Francisco campus.

Be sure to visit the Gleason Library at the University of San Francisco. The Sutro Collection of Judaica contains an extensive collection of Hebrew and medieval Judeo-Arabic manuscripts. Half of the collection was destroyed in the 1906 earthquake and fire, but the remainder still makes up the foremost collection of medieval Jewish manuscripts in the West.

CONGREGATION EMANU-EL

Arguello Boulevard & Lake Street   Tel. (415) 751-2535

The first religious service which the Jewish pioneers held on the shores of San Francisco Bay was in 1849. The following year, a new congregation was formed under the leadership of Emanuel Berg. In his honor the congregation was named Emanu-El. The membership numbered less than fifty when the congregation rented a hall for religious services on Bush Street, between Montgomery and Sansone Streets. In 1854, Congregation Emanu-El decided to build a new edifice on a lot which was purchased on Broadway, between Powell and Mason Streets.

In 1856, certain changes in the ritual service were introduced, which turned the congregation from orthodoxy. But not until 1860, did the congregation follow the liberal Reform movement which was then rapidly spreading from Germany to America.

The Jewish population now numbered about 10,000 people and Emanu-El decided to move from the Broadway synagogue to 450 Sutter Street, where a new edifice was erected. This new temple was considered one of the most impressive and one of the three largest in the country.

Dr. Elkan Cohn became rabbi in 1860, and a year later the Sutter Street property was bought for $15,000 from B. Davidson, the San Francisco agent for Rothschild. The new temple was designed by William Patton in Neo-Gothic style. It rose 165 feet above grade and was capped with two golden globes. The temple was dedicated in 1866.

San Francisco's Temple Emanu-El was dedicated in 1866.

Temple Emanu-El following the 1906 earthquake and fire.
Courtesy, American Jewish Historical Society, Waltham, Mass.

Unique Ark in Temple Emanu-El, San Francisco.

The magnificent structure survived the earthquake of 1868 and the combined assault of quake and fire in 1906. The globes did fall off during the tremors and the interior was virtually gutted. Nevertheless, it was rebuilt and housed the congregation for the next twenty years. The Sutter Street temple was ultimately demolished to make way for a new medical building.

The present building of Congregation Emanu-El on Arguello Boulevard was dedicated in 1926. The architecture is Levantine, representing a fusion of architectural styles of the Mediterranean world based upon a Byzantine-Roman tradition. It was designed by architects Arthur Brown, Jr., John Bakewell, Jr., Sylvain Schnaittacher; interior decorator Bruce Porter; and consultants G. Albert Lansburgh, Bernard B. Maybecy and Edgar Walter. The temple is built on an L-shaped lot, 288 feet on Arguello and 275 feet on Lake Street.

The exquisite Ark was built in London by two California artists, Frank Ingerson and George Dennison. It stands under a marble canopy and is made of bronze decorated with enamel and with symbols of the twelve tribes of Israel. It is fashioned like a jewel box, expressive of the precious nature of its contents, the Torah. Its dimensions are the same as those of the portable Ark carried by the ancient Jews in the wilderness before they entered the Promised Land.

Tours of the main sanctuary are conducted daily from 1:00 to 3:30 p.m.

HOLOCAUST MEMORIAL

A sculpture by George Segal was installed in Lincoln Park in 1984. The haunting bronze memorial depicts ten bodies heaped on the ground with a figure standing nearby in prison clothes peering through a barbed-wire fence.

SAN FRANCISCO CABLE CAR MUSEUM
1201 Mason Street   Tel. (415) 474-1887

San Francisco's cable cars are actually motorless "dummy" cars. They ride on typical trolley tracks. Between the tracks is a groove. Several inches below the surface is a continuously running cable. There is a metal "grip-arm" which surrounds the moving cable. When the conductor wishes to proceed, he switches the levers and the grip-arm latches onto the continuously moving cable. The cable moves at a constant 9.5 miles per hour. This constant momentum enables the cable car to climb up the 45-degree-angled hills of San Francisco. When the conductor wishes to stop the cable car, he releases the grip-arm from that moving cable and applies the brakes.

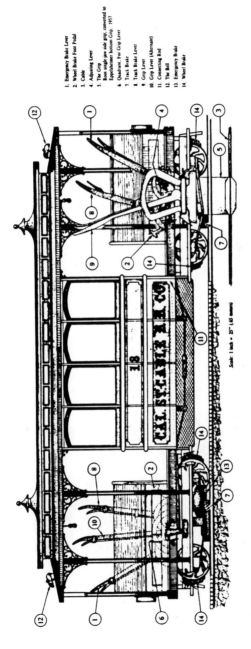

SAN FRANCISCO CABLE CARS

Section view of San Francisco's cable car.

1. Emergency Brake Lever
2. Wheel Brake Foot Pedal
3. Cable
4. Adjusting Lever
5. The Grip
   Boot single-jaw side grip; converted to Eppelsheimer bottom Grip, 1957
6. Quadrant, For Grip Lever
7. Track Brake
8. Track Brake Lever
9. Grip Lever
10. Grip Lever (Alternate)
11. Connecting Rod
12. The Bell
13. Emergency Brake
14. Wheel Brake

Scale: 1 inch = 25" (.65 mm)

San Leandro

OLDEST SYNAGOGUE IN CALIFORNIA
642 Dolores Avenue   Tel. (415) 357-8505

The San Leandro Hebrew Congregation was organized in 1886. Its original wood-frame one-story building was built in 1889 and was brought from its original site to the backyard of the present Temple Beth Sholom in 1953. The City of San Leandro, located just south of Oakland, has preserved the original small frame building as a city landmark. It is the oldest surviving synagogue structure in California.

The "Little Shul" now stands alongside a *Gan Tanachi* (Biblical Garden) and a permanent Sukkah on the Temple grounds. It is used frequently for various small functions of the congregation.

Temple Beth Sholom, San Leandro.

WINDMILLS, WINDMILLS, WINDMILLS
(ALAMEDA PASS)

As you drive east along Freeway 580 going toward Stockton, you will notice white propellers perched atop steel posts. These are modern-day windmills which generate electricity. They are located on the upper rims of a mountain range. It is as if you are looking at a surreal painting. The high-tech windmills sitting in a green pasture with cows grazing alongside.

There are several thousand windmills which are owned and/or leased by the Pacific Power & Electric Company. There are several varieties of windmills. Most are the propeller-types. Others are designed like king-size egg beaters! This, along with the one located in the Mohave Desert, is the largest windmill farm in the world.

Simi Valley

BRANDEIS-BARDIN INSTITUTE
1101 Pepper Tree Lane   (93064)   Tel. (805) 526-1131

The Brandeis-Bardin Institute, located on 3,200 acres in Simi Valley, is a "laboratory for living Judaism" offering creative programs for children, students and adults. Each summer, Brandeis sponsors two four-week sessions known as *aliyot*, bringing together young adults between ages 18 and 25 from around the world. Brandeis combines the models of the kibbutz, the Danish folk high school and American camping, and the program includes work, study, prayer and social activities. Outstanding Jewish personalities are present to discuss contemporary issues and instill within participants an appreciation for Judaism.

The landscape in the Simi Valley closely resembles that of Israel. This is the largest Jewish-owned property used for a Jewish "project" outside the State of Israel. The noted movie star, James Arness, who was not Jewish, was greatly impressed with Mr. Bardin's plan and donated 1100 acres to the Institute. He "threw in" his "ranch hand," who still lives near the stables.

The House of the Book, located on top of one of the mountains at Brandeis, was designed by architect Sidney Eisenshtat in 1964. This building serves as the synagogue. The building consists of a poured-concrete cluster of drums of varying heights. They are monumental in their unique sculptural shapes. The main entrance portrays a relief map of the City of Jerusalem.

How to get there: Take the San Diego Freeway (405) north from Los Angeles to Route 118, go west for about 15 miles and proceed to the second exit in Simi Valley.

Venice

PACIFIC JEWISH CENTER
505 Ocean Front Walk   (90291)   Tel. (213) 392-1707

Along the boardwalk there is a continuous streetfair of roller skaters, craft vendors, street entertainers and sidewalk cafes. This area was once a rundown slum with many elderly Jews living in the low-rent former resort. It has recently been restored and has become a "yuppified" (young urban professionals) area.

Some of the noted members of the congregation include Elliot Gould and Barbara Streisand. A Bar Mitzvah ceremony was planned for the late 92-year-old philanthropist and president of Occidental Petroleum, Armand Hammer. But, just a week before the ceremony, he passed away. A special Bar Mitzvah certificate, which was to be presented at the ceremony, now hangs along the "mizrach" (Eastern) wall of the synagogue.

GOLD RUSH - JEWISH HISTORIC SITES

Antioch

Mark S. Levy Store Front   *701 Second Street*   (1872)

Big Oak Flat

M. Gilbert Store, now 100F Lodge Hall (1850s)

Chinese Camp

Rosenbloom Store Ruins   (1850s)

Clayton

Clayton Hotel, founded by by Jacob Rhine,
now Pioneer Inn   (1850s)

Columbia

Levy Brothers Dry Goods   (1850s)

Downieville

Meier Building   (1850s)

Fiddletown

Randall Building

Folsom

Cohen Mansion   *Peddlers Lane & Scott Street*   (1890s)

Hyman House   *603 Figueroa Street*   (1860)

Lakeside Cemetery   (1861)

Edward Levy House   *Scott & Figueroa Streets*   (1869)

Grass Valley

Jewish cemetery   (1850s)

Wilson & Blossom Lane (Eureka Heights)

Jackson

Jewish cemetery   (1857)

Synagogue site   *Church & North Streets*

Jenny Lind

Rosenberg Store

Julian

Marks Building   *Washington & Main Streets*   (1886)

Livermore

Philip Ansbacher Residence   *879 South L Street*   (1869)

Marysville

Jewish cemetery   *Route 70*   (1850s)

Mokelumne Hill

L. Mayer & Son Store   (1854)

Jewish cemetery   (1850s)

Mountain View

Baer's Store   *Washington Street*   (1850s)

S. Weilheimer & Son General Store

124 & 128 Castro Street   (1859)

Nevada City

Aaron Baruch House   *516 Main Street*   (1852)

Jewish cemetery   Lower Grass Valley   (1854)

Oroville

Jewish cemetery

Feather River Boulevard & Mitchel Avenue   (1862)

Pittsburgh

Senderman & Israel Store

4th & Railroad Avenue   (1870s)

Placerville

Jewish cemetery   *Myrtle Avenue*   (1856)

Old synagogue   *Mill & Colma Streets*

Pomona

Philip's House   *2640 West Pomona Boulevard*   (1875)

Sacramento

First synagogue plaque   *7th & Capitol (L) Streets*

Jewish cemetery

   Stockton Boulevard & Lemon Hill Road   (1850s)

San Jose

Historic synagogue plaque   *Third & San Antonio Streets*

San Louis Obispo

Sinsheimer Brothers Store   *849 Monterey Street*   (1876)

Santa Cruz

Jewish cemetery   *Meder & Bay Streets*   (1877)

Shasta

Jewish cemetery - Pioneer Baby's Grave   *Route 299*   (1864)

Sonora

Baer's Store   *Washington Street*   (1851)

Jewish cemetery   *Yaney Avenue & Oak Street*   (1853)

Stockton

Jewish cemetery   (1851)   *Union, Poplar & Acadia Streets*

Temecula

Wolf's General Store   *Route 71*

Vallecito

Moses Dinklespiel's Store   (1850s)

KOSHER PROVISIONS

Encino

Kinneret
18046 Ventura Boulevard   Tel. (818) 609-0599
Simon's Restaurant
17614 Ventura Boulevard   Tel. (818) 995-1484
La Jolla
Western Kosher
7739 Fay Avenue   Tel. (619) 454-6328
Los Angeles
Beverly Grand Hotel   (Shabbat meals)
7257 Beverly Boulevard   Tel. (213) 939-1653
Beverly Hills Patisserie
9100 West Pico Boulevard   Tel. 275-6873
Chick-A-Deli
7170 Beverly Boulevard   Tel. 932-0674
China On Rye
9407 West Pico Boulevard   Tel. 556-8207
Dan Michael's
7777 Sunset Boulevard   Tel. 851-7557
Eilat Bakery
9233 West Pico Boulevard   Tel. 205-8700
Elite Cuisine
7117 Beverly Boulevard   Tel. 930-1303
Fairfax Kosher Pizza
453 North Fairfax Avenue   Tel. 653-7200
Fish Grill
7226 Beverly Boulevard   Tel. 937-7162
The Fishing Well
8975 West Pico Boulevard   Tel. 859-9429
Judy's Grill
129 North La Brea Avenue   Tel. 936-1551

Kosher Kolonel
9301 West Pico Boulevard   Tel. 858-0111
Kosher Nostra
365 South Fairfax Avenue   Tel. 655-1994
Little Jerusalem
8971 West Pico Boulevard   Tel. 858-8361
Micheline's   (Mexican)
8965 West Pico Boulevard   Tel. 274-6534
The Milky Way
9107 West Pico Boulevard   Tel. 859-0004
Olé   (Mexican)
7912 Beverly Boulevard   Tel. 933-7254
Pat's Restaurant   (Italian)
9233 West Pico Boulevard   Tel. 205-8705
Peking Tam   (Chinese)
363 South Fairfax Avenue   Tel. 658-8118
Pepe Tam   (Mexican)
9411 West Pico Boulevard   Tel. 556-3535
Serravalle (French)
8837 West Pico Boulevard   Tel. 550-8372
Simon's Restaurant   (Persian)
8706 West Pico Boulevard   Tel. 657-5552
Western Kosher   (Mexican)
426 North Fairfax Avenue   Tel. 655-8870
North Hollywood
Drexler's Restaurant
12519 1/2 Burbank Boulevard   Tel. (818) 984-1160
Hadar   (Ethiopian)
12514 Burbank Boulevard   Tel. 762-1155
La Pizza Ristorante
12515 Burbank Boulevard   Tel. 760-8198
Nosh & Rye
12422-24 Burbank Boulevard   Tel. 760-7694

Oakland
Oakland Kosher Foods
3256 Grand Avenue   Tel. (415) 451-3883
Holy Land Deli
677 Rand Avenue   Tel. (415) 272-0535

Palm Springs
L & H Kosher Foods
618 East Sunny Dunes   Tel. (619) 320-6610

Palo Alto
Mollie Stone's Markets
164 South California Avenue   Tel. (415) 323-8361

Sacramento
Bob's Butcher Block & Deli
6436 Fair Oaks Boulevard   Tel. (916) 482-6884

San Diego
Lang's Loaf
6165 El Cajon Boulevard, Suite E
Campus Plaza Center   Tel. (619) 287-7306

San Francisco
B'nai B'rith Hillel Foundation
(Sabbath meals only - when school is in session)
33 Banbury Drive   Tel. (415) 333-4922
Israel Kosher Market
5621 Geary Street   Tel. 752-3064
Lotus Garden
(Vegetarian cuisine under local rabbinical supervision)
532 Grant Avenue   (Chinatown)   Tel. 397-0707
Natan's Grill & Restaurant
420 Geary Street   (Downtown)   Tel. 776-2683
Tel Aviv Kosher Market
1301 Noriega Street   Tel. 661-7588

San Jose
Willow Glen Deli
1185 Lincoln Avenue   Tel. (408) 297-6604

Walnut Creek

Pita King

1607 Palos Verdes Mall   Tel. (415) 945-0386

SYNAGOGUES

Agoura Hills 91301

Chabad House (O)

68 North Canan Road *Tel. (818) 991-0991*

Alameda 94501

Temple Israel (R)

3183 McCartney Road *Tel. (415) 522-9355*

Alhambra 91801

Temple Beth Torah (C)

225 South Atlantic Boulevard *Tel. (818) 284-0296*

Anaheim 92804

Temple Beth Emeth (C)

1770 West Cerritos Avenue *Tel. (714) 772-4720*

Chabad House (O)

1335 South Euclid Avenue *Tel. 520-0770*

Anaheim Hills 92807

Chabad House (O)

1265 North Schrisdey #A203 *Tel. (714) 693-0770*

Aptos 95003

Temple Beth El (R)

3055 Porter Gulch Road *Tel. (408) 479-3444*

Arcadia 91006

Temple Shaarei Tikvah (C)

550 South 2nd Avenue *Tel. (818) 445-0810*

Arleta 91331

Temple Beth Sholom of the Deaf (R)

13580 Osborne Street *Tel. (818) 899-2202*

Bakersfield 93305

Temple Beth El (R)

2906 Loma Linda Drive *Tel. (805) 322-7607*

Congregation B'nai Jacob (C)

600 17th Street *Tel. 325-8017*

Barstow   92311
Congregation Beth Israel   (R)
428 Highland   Tel. (619) 256-5552
Bel Air   90077
Chabad of Bel Air   (O)
10421 Summer Holly Circle   Tel. (213) 475-5311
Leo Baeck Temple   (R)
1300 North Sepulveda Boulevard   Tel. 476-2861
Stephen S. Wise Temple   (R)
15500 Stephen S. Wise Drive   Tel. 476-8651
University Synagogue   (R)
11960 Sunset Boulevard   Tel. 272-3650
Belmont
Peninsula Jewish Community Center
2440 Carlmont Drive
Berkeley   94708
Berkeley Hillel Foundation
2736 Bancroft Way   Tel. (415) 845-7793
Congregation Beth El   (R)
2301 Vine Street   Tel. (415) 848-3988
Congregation Beth Israel   (O)
1630 Bancroft Way   Tel. 843-5246
Chabad House of Berkeley   (O)
2643 College Avenue   Tel. 540-5824
Kehilla Community Synagogue
Unitarian Universalist Fellowship
Cedar & Bonita Roads   Tel. 654-5452
Congregation Netivot Shalom   (C)
Berkely/ Richmond JCC   1414 Walnut Street   Tel. 527-9730
Beverly Hills   90211
Congregation Beth Jacob   (O)
9030 Olympic Boulevard   Tel. (213) 278-1911
Chabad of North Beverly Hills   (O)
409 Foothill Road   Tel. 271-9063

Temple Emanu-El   (R)

300 North Clark Drive   Tel. 274-6388

Temple Tanya   *133 South Almount Drive*

Young Israel   (O)   *8701 West Pico Boulevard   Tel. 275-3020*

Brentwood

Chabad of Brentwood   (O)

11922 San Vicente Boulevard   Tel. (213) 826-4453

Burbank   91505

Temple Beth Emet-Burbank   (R)

600 North Buena Vista Avenue   Tel. (818) 843-4787

Congregation B'nai Emunah   (T)

4001 West Magnolia Boulevard   Tel. 842-6412

Temple Emanu-El   (C)

1302 North Glenoaks Boulevard   Tel. 845-1734

Burlingame   94010

Peninsula Temple Sholom   (R)

1655 Sebastian Drive   Tel. (415) 697-2266

Canoga Park   91307

Congregation Beth Kodesh   (C)

7401 Shoup Avenue   Tel. (818) 346-0811

Temple Solael of Woodland Hills   (R)

6601 Valley Circle Boulevard   Tel. 348-3885

West Park Jewish Community Center

22622 Van Owen Street

Carmel   93923

Congregation Beth Israel   (R)

5716 Carmel Valley Road   Tel. (408) 375-2759

Castro Valley   94546

Congregation Shir Ami   (R)

4529 Malabar Avenue   Tel. (415) 537-1787

Cathedral City

Temple Sinai of the Desert   *Chuerosa Lane*

Chatsworth   91311

Valley Outreach Synagogue

10410 De Soto Avenue   Tel. (818) 998-8410

Chico   95927
Congregation Beth Israel   (R)
1336 Hemlock Street   Tel. (916) 342-6146
China Lake   93555
Beth Torah **Naval** Weapons Center   (R)
All-Faith Chapel   Tel. (619) 939-3506
Chula Vista   92010
Temple Beth Sholom   (C)
208 Madrona Avenue   Tel. (619) 420-6040
Beth Torah Congregation   (O)
380 Telegraph Canyon Road   Tel. 427-9820
Citrus Heights   95611
Sunrise Jewish Congregation   (R)
P.O.Box 405   Tel. (916) 965-8322
Concord
Congregation Beth Am   *996 Oak Grove*
Corona   91720
Temple Beth Sholom   (C)   *823 Sheridan Street*
Costa Mesa   92627
Temple Sharon   (C)
617 West Hamilton Street   Tel. (714) 631-3262
Culver City   90230
Temple Akiba   (R)
5249 South Sepulveda Boulevard   Tel. (213) 870-6575
Cupertino
Congregation Beth David   *11100 South Sterling Road*
Daly City   94015
Congregation B'nai Israel   (C)
1575 Annie Street   Tel. (415)756-5430
Davis   95616
Jewish Fellowship of Davis   (R)
1821 Oak Avenue   Tel. (916) 758-0842
Desert Hot Springs   92240
Temple Neve Sholom   (C)
66-777 East Pierson Boulevard   Tel. (619) 329-5168

Downey   90241

Temple Ner Tamid   (R)

   10629 Lakewood Boulevard   Tel. (213) 861-9276

El Centro

Congregation Beth Jacob   *530 Adams Avenue*

El Monte

B'nai Israel Temple   *733 North Tyler*

El Toro

Temple Eilat   *24432 Murlands*

Encinitas   92024

Temple Solel   (R)

   552 South El Camino Real   Tel. (619) 436-0654

Encino   91436

Chabad of the Valley   (O)

   4915 Havenhurst Avenue   Tel. (818) 784-9985

Temple Judea   (R)   *5429 Lindley Avenue   Tel. 987-2616*

Temple Ner Maariv   (C)

   5180 Yarmouth Avenue   Tel. 345-7833

Shir Chadash New Reform Temple   (R)

   17000 Ventura Boulevard   Tel. 986-6102

Maariv Temple   (C)   *5180 Yarmouth Avenue   Tel. 345-7833*

Valley Beth Shalom   (C)

   15739 Ventura Boulevard   Tel. 872-1360

Eureka   95502

Temple Beth El   (R)

   Hodgson & T Streets   Tel. (707) 444-2846

Fontana   92335

Temple Israel (C)   *14795 Merrill Strteet*

Foster City

Peninsula Sinai Congregation

   Edgewater Boulevard & Boothbay Avenue

Fountain Valley

Congregation B'nai Tzedek   *18225 Bushard Avenue*

Fremont   94538

Temple Beth Torah   (R)
                42000 Paseo Padre Parkway   Tel. (415) 656-7141
Fresno   93715
 Temple Beth Israel   (R)
                2336 Calavaras Street   Tel. (209) 264-2929
Congregation Beth Jacob   (C)
                    406 West Shields Avenue   Tel. 222-0664
Fullerton   92631
 Temple Beth Tikvah   (R)
                1600 North Acadia Avenue   Tel. (714) 871-3535
Gardenia   90249
Southwest Temple Beth Torah   (C)
                14725 South Gramercy Place   Tel. (213) 327-8734
Glendale   91202
Temple Sinai   (R)
                1212 North Pacific Avenue   Tel. (818) 246-8101
Granada Hills
Temple Beth Torah   (R)
                16651 Rinaldi Street   Tel. (818) 831-0835
North Valley Jewish Community Center   *16601 Rinaldi Street*
Guerneville   95446
Russian River Jewish Community
                    P.O.Box 2274   Tel. (707) 887-9540
Hanford
 Congregation B'nai David
Hesperia   92345
Bamidbar Shel Ma'alah   (R)
                    P.O.Box 1397   Tel. (619) 244-8623
Huntington Beach   92649
Chabad House   (O)
                5702 Clark Drive #18   Tel. (714) 846-2285
Huntington Park   90255
 Huntington Park Hebrew Congregation   (C)
                2877 East Florence Avenue   Tel. (213) 585-4436

Irvine
Beth Jacob Congregation   (O)
                    3415 Michelson   Tel. (714) 786-5230
Chabad House   (O)
                    4872 Royce Road El   Tel. (714) 786-5000
Lafayette   94549
Temple Isaiah   (R)
                    3800 Mt. Diablo Boulevard   Tel. (415) 283-8575
Laguna Beach
Chabad House   (O)   *P.O.Box 253   Tel. (714) 786-5000*
Laguna Hills
Temple Judea   *24512 Moulton Parkway   Tel. (714) 830-0470*
La Jolla   92037
 Congregation Beth Am   (C)
                    525 Stevens Avenue   Tel. (619) 481-8454
Congregation Beth El   (C)   *8660 Gilman Road   Tel. 452-1734*
Chabad House   (O)
            8950 Villa La Jolla Drive, Suite 1225   Tel. 455-1670
 La Mirada   90638
 Temple Beth Ohr   (R)
                15721 East Rosecrans Avenue   Tel. (714) 521-6765
Lakewood   90713
Temple Beth Zion-Sinai   (C)
                6440 Del Ami Boulevard   Tel. (213) 429-1014
Lancaster   93534
 Beth Kneseth Bamidbar   (R)
                    1611 East Avenu J   Tel. (805) 942-4415
Congregation B'nai Israel   (C)
                    43652 Higbee Avenue   Tel. 945-2296
Livermore   94550
 Congregation Beth Emek   (R)
                    1886 College Avenue   Tel. (415) 443-1689
Lomita
Chabad House   (O)
                    24412 Narbonne Avenue   Tel. (213) 326-8234

Long Beach   90814

Temple Beth Shalom   (C)

3635 Elm Avenue   Tel. (213) 426-6413

Temple Israel   (R)   *3538 East 3rd Street   Tel. 434-0996*

Chabad House   (O)   *3981 Atlantic Avenue   Tel. 434-6338*

Young Israel of Long Beach   (O)

4134 Atlantic Avenue   Tel. 426-9690

Los Altos Hills   94022

Congregation Beth Am   (R)

26790 Arastradero Road   Tel. (415) 493-4661

Los Angeles   90048

Congregation Adat Shalom   (C)

3030 Westwood Boulevard   Tel. (213) 475-4985

Congregation Agudath Israel   (O)

7114 Rosewood Avenue   Tel. 930-0792

Ahavas Yisroel Synagogue   (O)

729 La Brea Avenue   Tel. 857-1607

Ahavath Israel Congregation   (O)

5452 Virginia Avenue   Tel. 464-3855

Temple Akiba   (R)

5249 South Sepulveda Boulevard   Tel. 870-6575

Anshei Emeth Synagogue   (O)

1490 South Robertson Boulevard   Tel. 275-5640

Temple Beth Am   (C)

1039 South La Cienega Boulevard   Tel. 652-7353

Congregation Beth Chayim Chadashim   (R)

6000 West Pico Boulevard   Tel. 931-7023

Hollywood Temple Beth El   (C)

1317 North Crescent Heights Boulevard   Tel. 656-3150

Congregation Beth Israel   (O)

8058 Beverly Boulevard   Tel. 651-4022

Temple Beth Israel of Highland Park   (C)

5711 Monte Vista   Tel. 255-5416

Temple Beth Torah   (C)

11827 Venice Boulevard   Tel. 398-4536

Temple Beth Zion   (C)
5555 West Olympic Boulevard   Tel. 933-9136
B'nai David-Judea Congregation   (T)
8906 West Pico Boulevard   Tel. 272-7223
B'nai Tikvah Congregation   (C)
5820 Manchester Avenue   Tel. 645-6262
Breed Street Shul (Cong. Talmud Torah)   (O)
247 North Breed Street   Tel. 262-3922
Chabad House   (O)   741 Gayley Avenue   Tel. 208-7511
Chabad House   (O)
3355 Manning Avenue #17   Tel. 837-4941
Chabad House   (O)
11920 San Vincente Boulevard   Tel. 826-4453
Chabad House-Russian Synagogue   (O)
221 South La Brea Avenue   Tel. 938-1837
Chabad of Cheviot Hills   (O)
3268 Motor Avenue   Tel. 474-6685
Congregation Chofetz Chaim   (O)
7353 West Beverly Boulevard
Etz Jacob Congregation   (O)
7659 Beverly Boulevard   Tel. 938-2619
Ezrat Israel Congregation   (C)
447 North Fairfax Avenue   Tel. 651-2227
Hollywood Temple Beth El   (C)
1317 North Crescent Heights Boulevard   Tel. 656-3150
Temple Isaiah   (R)
10345 West Pico Boulevard   Tel. 277-2772
Temple Israel of Hollywood   (R)
7300 Hollywood Boulevard   Tel. 876-8330
Kahal Joseph Congregation   (O)
10505 Santa Monica Boulevard   Tel. 474-0559
Congregation Kehilat Yitzchok   (O)
7709 Beverly Boulevard   Tel. 932-8694
Kehillat Ma'ariv Congregation   (C)
12000 San Vicente   Tel. 826-6355

Knesseth Israel Congregation   (O)
>   2364 South Robertson Boulevard   Tel. 839-4962

Knesseth Israel of Hollywood   (C)
>   1260 North Vermont Avenue   Tel. 665-5171

Leo Baeck Temple   (R)
>   1300 North Sepulveda Boulevard   Tel. 476-2861

Congregation Magen Abraham   (O)
>   356 North La Brae Avenue   Tel. 932-9690

Congregation Magen David   (T)
>   9717 West Pico Boulevard   Tel. 879-3861

Midrash Od Yosef Chai   (T)
>   420 North Fairfax Avenue   Tel. 653-5163

Congregation Mishkan Israel   (O)
>   8237 West 3rd Street   Tel. 655-3133

Congregation Ner Israel   (O)
>   219 South Alta Vista Boulevard   Tel. 933-3405

Congregation Netzach Israel   (O)
>   4117 Beverly Boulevard   Tel. 665-4757

Congregation Ohel David   (O)
>   7967 Beverly Boulevard   Tel. 651-3594

Congregation Ohel Yosef Yitzchok   (Chabad)   (O)
>   1017 Havenhurst Boulevard   Tel. 650-4765

Ohev Sholom Congregation   (O)
>   525 South Fairfax Avenue   Tel. 653-7190

Congregation Ohr Chaim Shapiro   (O)
>   960 North Martel Avenue   Tel. 874-6656

Sephardic Congregation Kehal Yoseph   (O)
>   10505 Santa Monica Boulevard   Tel. 474-0559

Sephardic Hebrew Center   (C)
>   4911 West 59th Street   Tel. 295-5541

Sephardic Magen David Congregation   (O)
>   7454 Melrose Avenue   Tel. 655-3441

Sephardic Temple Tifereth Israel   (O)
>   10500 Wilshire Boulevard   Tel. 475-7311

Congregation Shaarei Tefila   (O)

7269 Beverly Boulevard   Tel. 938-7147

Temple Shir Shalom   (R)

3590 South Grandview Boulevard   Tel. 391-2660

Sinai Temple   (C)   *10400 Wilshire Boulevard   Tel. 474-1518*

Stephen S. Wise Temple   (R)

15500 Stephen S. Wise Drive   Tel. 476-8561

Synagogue for the Performing Arts   (C/R)

1727 Barrington Court, Suite 205   Tel. 472-3500

Congregation Tifereth Zvi   (O)

7561 Beverly Boulevard   Tel. 931-3252

Congregation Torah Vechesed   (O)

6407 West Orange Street   Tel. 657-3689

University Synagogue   (R)

11960 Sunset Boulevard   Tel. 472-1255

Wilshire Boulevard Temple   (R)

3663 Wilshire Boulevard   Tel. 388-2401

Yeshiva Rav Isaacsohn Torah Emeth Academy   (O)

540 North La Brea Avenue   Tel. 939-1148

Young Israel of Century City   (O)

9317 West Pico Boulevard   Tel. 273-6954

Young Israel of Hancock Park   (O)

225 South La Brea Avenue   Tel. 931-4030

Young Israel of Los Angeles   (O)

660 North Spaulding   Tel. 655-0300

Los Gatos   95032

Congregation Shir Hadash   (R)

16555 Shannon Road   Tel. (408) 358-1751

Malibu

Malibu Jewish Center   (Rec)

3504 Winter Canyon Road   Tel. (213) 456-2178

Merced   95344

Congregation Etz Chaim   (R)

P.O.Box 2531   Tel. (209) 722-0530

Marina Del Ray   90292
Chabad House   (O)
                        714 Washington Street   Tel. (213) 306-0744
Mission Viejo   92692
Temple Beth El   (R)
                        28892 Marguerite Parkway   Tel. (714) 364-2332
Temple Eilat   (C)   *22081 Hidalgo   Tel. 770-9606*
Modesto   95350
Congregation Beth Shalom   (C)
                        1705 Sherwood Avenue   Tel. (209) 522-5613
Montebello   90640
Temple B'nai Emet   (C)
                        482 North Garfield Avenue   Tel. (213) 723-2978
Murrieta Hot Springs   92362
Congregation B'nai Chaim   (C)
                        29500 Via Princesa   Tel. (714) 677-7350
Napa   94558
Congregation Beth Sholom   (C)
                        1455 Elm Street   Tel. (707) 255-9800
Newhall
Congregation Beth Shalom   (C)
                        23045 Lyons Avenue   Tel. (805) 254-2411
Newport Beach   92660
Temple Bat Yahm   (R)
                        1011 Camelback Street   Tel. (714) 644-1999
Temple Isaiah   (C)   *2401 Irvine Street   Tel. 548-6900*
Harbor Reform Temple   (R)
                        2100A Mar Vista   Tel. 644-7230
North Hollywood   91607
Congregation Adat Ari El   (C)
                        5540 Laurel Canyon Boulevard   Tel. (818) 766-9426
Adat Yeshurun Sephardic Congregation   (O)
                        6348 Whitsett Avenue   Tel. (818) 766-4682
Aish Hatorah Institute   (O)
                        12422 Chandler Boulevard   Tel. 980-6934

Temple Beth Hillel   (R)

12326 Riverside Drive   Tel. 877-3431

Chabad of North Hollywood   (O)

13079 Chandler Boulevard   Tel. 989-9539

Em Habanim Sephardic Congregation   (O)

5850 Laurel Canyon Boulevard   Tel. 762-7779

Kehillath Ma'ariv, The Westside Congregation   (C)

1715 21st Street   Tel. (213) 829-0566

Shaarey Zedek Congregation   (O)

12800 Chandler Boulevard   Tel. 763-0560

Valley Mishkan Israel Congregation   (O)

6450 Bellingham Avenue   Tel. 769-8043

Young Israel of North Hollywood   (O)

P.O.Box 4827   (91617)

Northridge   91324

Temple Ahavat Shalom   (R)

18200 Rinaldi Place   Tel. (818) 360-2258

Temple Ramat Zion   (C)

17655 Devonshire Street   Tel. 360-1881

Young Israel of Northridge   (O)   Tel. 368-2221

Novato   94948

Congregation Beth El   (R)

P.O.Box 494   Tel. (414) 257-5406

Oakland   94610

Temple Beth Abraham   (C)

327 MacArthur Boulevard   Tel. (415) 832-0936

Beth Jacob Congregation   (O)

3778 Park Boulevard   Tel. 482-1147

Temple Sinai   (R)   2808 Summit Street   Tel. 451-3263

Ontario   91762

Temple Sholom   (C)

963 West 6th Street   Tel. (714) 983-9661

Pacific Palisades   90272

Kehilath Israel   (Rec)

16019 Sunset Boulevard   Tel. (213) 459-2328

Palm Desert 92260
Temple Sinai (R)
43-435 Monterey Avenue Tel. (619) 568-9699
Palm Springs 92262
Temple Isaiah (O/C/R)
332 West Alejo Road Tel. 3(619) 25-2281
Temple N'vey Shalom
86777 East Pierson Boulevard Tel. 329-5168
The Desert Synagogue Kehillat Hamidbar (O)
1068 North Palm Canyon Drive Tel. 327-4848
Palo Alto 94306
Chabad House (O)   *3070 Louis Road Tel. (415) 424-9800*
Congregation Kol Emeth (C)
4175 Manuela Avenue Tel. 948-7498
Palo Alto Orthodox Minyan (O)
453 Sherman Avenue Tel. 326-5001
Pasadena 91107
Pasadena Jewish Temple (C)
1434 North Altadena Drive Tel. (818) 798-1161
Petaluma 94952
Congregation B'nai Israel (C)
740 Western Avenue Tel. (707) 762-9976
Pomona 91767
Temple Beth Israel (R)
3033 North Towne Avenue Tel. (714) 626-1277
Poway 92064
Temple Adat Shalom (R)
15905 Pomerado Road Tel. (619) 451-1200
Chabad House (O)   *16934 Espola Road Tel. 451-0455*
Ramona 92065
Congregation Etz Chaim (R)
P.O.Box 1138 Tel. (619) 789-7393
Rancho Palos Verdes 90274
Congregation Ner Tamid (C)
5721 Crestridge Road Tel. (213) 377-6986

Redding   96099

Congregation Beth Israel   (R)

P.O.Box 201   Tel. (916) 244-2278

Redondo Beach   90277

Temple Menorah   (R)

1101 Camino Real   Tel. (213) 316-8444

Redwood City   94061

Temple Beth Jacob   (C)

1550 Alameda de las Plugas   Tel. (415) 366-8481

Reseda

Temple Beth Ami   (C)

18449 Kittridge Street   Tel. (818) 343-4624

Richmond   94803

Temple Beth Hillel   (R)

801 Park Central   Tel. (415) 223-2560

Riverside   92506

Temple Beth El   (R)

2675 Central Avenue   Tel. (714) 684-4511

Rolling Hills Estate   90274

Chabad House   (O)

777 Silver Spur Road #12B   Tel. (213) 544-5544

Sacramento   95818

Congregation B'nai Israel   (R)

3600 Riverside Boulevard   Tel. 446-4861

Knesseth Israel Torah Center   (O)

1024 Morse Avenue   Tel. 481-1159

Mosaic Law Congregation   (C)

2300 Sierra Boulevard   Tel. 488-1122

Salinas   93901

Temple Beth El   (R)

1212 South Riker Street   Tel. (408) 424-9151

San Bernardino   92405

Temple Emanu-El   (R)

3512 North E Street   Tel. (714) 886-4818

San Carlos
Tifereth Israel Synagogue   *7890 Tommy Drive*
San Diego   92103
Congregation Beth Israel   (R)
                                    2512 Third Avenue   Tel. (619) 239-0149
Beth Jacob Congregation   (O)
                                    4855 College Avenue   Tel. 287-9890
Congregation Beth Tefilah   (C)
                                    4967 69th Street   Tel. 463-0391
Chabad House   (O)   *6115 Montezuma Road   Tel. 265-7700*
Temple Emanu-El   (R)   *6299 Capri Drive   Tel. 286-2555*
Congregation Or El   (C)   *2512 Third Avenue   Tel. 239-1065*
Tifereth Israel Synagogue   (C)
                    6660 Cowles Mountain Boulevard   Tel. 697-6001
San Francisco   94118
Congregation Adath Israel   (O)
                                    1851 Noriega Street   Tel. (415) 564-5665
Congregation Anshei Ha'sefer
                                    1185 Vicente Street   Tel. 661-3347
Congregation Anshey Sfard   (O)
                                    1500 Clement Street   Tel. 752-4979
Congregation Beth Israel-Judea   (C/R)
                                    625 Brotherhood Way   Tel. 586-8833
Congregation Beth Sholom   (C)
                        14th Avenue & Clement Street   Tel. 221-8736
Congregation B'nai Emunah   (C)
                                    3595 Taraval Street   Tel. 664-7373
Chabad-Downtown   (O)
            11 Tillman Place   Tel. 956-8644   (weekdays only)

Congregation Chevra Tehilim   (O)
                                    751 25th Avenue   Tel. 752-2866
Congregation Emanu-El   (R)
                Arguello Boulevard & Lake Street   Tel. 751-2535

Fog City Egalitarian Minyan
San Francisco Hillel   33 Banbury Drive   Tel. 681-8098
Congregation Keneseth Israel   (O)
655 Sutter Street, Suite 203   Tel. 771-3420
(Sabbath services only)
Magen David Sephardic Congregation   (O)
351 4th Avenue   Tel. 752-9095
Congregation Ner Tamid   (C)
1250 Quintara Street   Tel. 661-3383
Richmond Torah Center   (O)
2440 Clement Street   Tel. 386-8123
Congregation Shaar Zahav   (R)
220 Danvers Street   Tel. 861-6932
Congregation Sherith Israel   (R)
2266 California Street   Tel. 346-1720
Congregation Torat Emeth   (O)
768 27th Avenue   Tel. 386-1830
Young Israel   (O)   1806-A Noriega Street   Tel. 752-7333
West Bay Havurah   2126 15th Street   Tel. 225-8830
San Jose   95153
Congregation Am Echad   (O)
1537A Meridian Avenue   Tel. (408) 267-2591
Temple Beth Sholom   (R)
325 Cheynoweth Avenue   Tel. 978-5566
Chabad House   (O)
1281 Juli Lynn Drive   Tel. 927-0766
Temple Emaun-El   (R)
1010 University Avenue   Tel. 292-0939
Congregation Sinai   (T)
1532 Willow Brea Avenue   Tel. 264-8542
Young Israel   (O)
1975 Hamilton Avenue   (Suite 5)   Tel. 559-6300
San Leandro   94577
Temple Beth Sholom   (C)
642 Dolores Avenue   Tel. (415) 357-8505

San Luis Obispo   93401
Congregation Beth David   (R)
2932 Augusta Street   Tel. (805) 544-0760
San Mateo   94403
Peninsula Temple Beth El   (R)
1700 Alameda de las Pulga   Tel. (415) 341-7701
Santa Monica   90401
Chabad House   (O)   *1428 17th Street   Tel. (213) 829-5620*
San Pedro   90732
Temple Beth El   (R)
1435 West 7th Street   Tel. (213) 833-2467
San Rafael   94903
Chabad House   (O)
37 Mount Whitney Drive   Tel. (415) 492-1666
Congregation Rodef Sholom   (R)
170 North San Pedro Road   Tel. 479-3441
Santa Ana   92705
Temple Beth Sholom   (R)
2625 North Tustin Avenue   Tel. (714) 532-6724
Santa Barbara   93111
Congregation B'nai B'rith   (R)
900 San Antonio Creek Road   Tel. (805) 964-7869
Chabad House   (O)
487 North Turnpike Road   Tel. (805) 683-1544
Young Israel of Santa Barbara   (O)
1826 "C" Cliff Drive (rear)   Tel. 966-1565
Santa Cruz   95060
Temple Beth El   (R)   *920 Bay Street   Tel. (408) 423-3012*
Santa Maria   93454
Temple Beth El   (R)
1501 East Alvin Avenue   Tel. (805) 928-2118
Santa Monica   90403
Bay Cities Chabad House   (O)
1428 17th Street   Tel. (213) 829-5620

Beth Sholom Temple   (R)

1827 California Avenue   Tel. 453-3361

Kehillath Ma'ariv, The Westside Congregation   (C)

1715 21st Street   Tel. (213) 829-0566

Santa Monica Synagogue   (R)

958 Lincoln Boulevard   Tel. 394-4594

Young Israel of Santa Monica   (O)

214 Marine Street   Tel. 399-5686

Santa Rosa   95405

Temple Beth Ami   (C)

4676 Mayette Avenue   Tel. (707) 545-4334

Shomrei Torah Congregation   (R)

1717 Yulupa Avenue   Tel. 578-5519

Saratoga   95070

Congregation Beth David   (C)

19700 Prospect Road   Tel. (408) 257-3333

Sepulveda   91343

Temple Beth Torah   (R)

8756 Woodley Avenue   Tel. (818) 893-3756

Sherman Oaks   91403

Temple B'nai Hayim   (C)

4302 Van Nuys Boulevard   Tel. (818) 788-4664

Chabad House   (O)

1463 Ventura Boulevard #202   Tel. 784-9985

Simi Valley   93062

Congregation B'nai Emet   (R)

P.O.Box 878   Tel. (805) 581-3723

Temple Ner Tamid   (C)

3050 Los Angeles Avenue   Tel. 522-4747

Sierra Madre

Foothill Jewish Community Center   *213 Lima Street*

Stockton   95207

Congregation Adas Yeshurun   (T)

427 East Fremont Street   Tel. (209) 478-4314

Temple Israel   (R)

5105 North El Dorado Street   Tel. 477-9306

Simi

Temple Ner Tamid-Simi   (C)

1122 Appleton Road   Tel. (805) 522-4747

Studio City   91604

Congregation Beth Meier   (C)

11725 Moorpark Street   Tel. (818) 769-0515

Congregation Beth Ohr

12355 Moorpark Street   Tel. 766-3826

Sun Valley   91352

Valley Beth Israel   (C)

16030 Roscoe Boulevard   Tel. (818) 782-2281

Tarzana   91356

Chabad of Tarzana (O)

18211 Burbank Boulevard   Tel. (818) 784-9985

Temple Judea   (R)   *5429 Lindley Avenue   Tel. 987-2616*

Congregation Or Ha'emek   (O)

5197 Garden Grove Avenue   Tel. 996-4627

Sephardic Cohen Synagogue   (O)

Nestle Avenue School   Tel. 789-2640

Temple City   91780

Temple Beth David   (R)

9677 Longden Avenue   Tel. (818) 287-9994

Thousand Oaks   91360

Temple Adath Elohim   (R)

2420 East Hillcrest Drive   Tel. (805) 497-7101

Temple Etz Chaim   (C)   *1080 Janss Road   Tel. 497-6891*

Tujunga   91040

Verdugo Hills Hebrew Center   (C)

10275 Tujunga Canyon Road   Tel. (818) 352-3171

Tustin

Congregation B'nai Israel   (C)

655 South B Street   Tel. (714) 730-9693

Valencia 91355

Temple Beth Ami   (R)

   24901 Orchard Village Road   Tel. (805) 259-7327

Vallejo 04590

Congregation B'nai Israel   (C)

   1256 Nebraska Street   Tel. (707) 642-6526

Van Nuys 91405

Temple Beth David   (C)   *7452 Hazeltine Avenue*

Chabad House   (O)

   13079 Chandler Boulevard   Tel. (818) 989-9539

Makon Ohr Shalom   *15339 Saticoy Street   Tel. 344-3113*

Temple Ner Tamid   (C)

   15339 Saticay Street   Tel. (818) 782-9010

Venice 90291

Congregation Mishkan Tephilo   (C)

   206 Main Street   Tel. (213) 392-3029

Pacific Jewish Center at Bay Cities Stnagogue   (T/O)

   505 Ocean Front Walk   Tel. 392-8749

Ventura 93004

Temple Beth Torah   (R)

   7620 Foothill Road   Tel. (805) 647-4181

Chabad House   (O)   *5850 Thille #101   Tel. 658-9127*

Visalia 93278

Congregation B'nai David   (R)

   P.O.Box 3822   Tel. (209) 732-3139

Vista 92083

Temple Judea   (C)   *1930 Sunset Drive   Tel. (619) 724-8318*

Walnut Creek 94598

Congregation Beth Am   (C)

   Contra Costa JCC

   2071 Tice Valley Road   Tel. (415) 493-4661

Congregation B'nai Sholom   (C)

   74 Eckley Lane   Tel. (415) 934-9446

Congregation B'nai Tikvah   (R)

   25 Hillcroft Way   Tel. (415) 933-5397

West Covina 91791

Temple Beth Ami   (C)

3508 East Temple Way   Tel. (818) 331-0515

Temple Shalom   (R)

1912 West Merced Avenue   Tel. 337-6500

West Hills 91307

Temple Solael   (R)

6601 Valley Circle Boulevard   Tel. (818) 348-3885

West Hollywood 90046

Chabad House   (O)

7414 Santa Monica Boulevard   Tel. (213) 874-7583

West Lake Village

Temple Adath Elohim   *1049 West Lake Boulevard*

Chabad House   (O)

741 Lakefield Road   (Suite E)   Tel. (805) 497-9635

West Los Angeles 90035

Chabad House   (O)

9017 West Pico Boulevard   Tel. (213) 271-6193

Westminster 92683

Temple Beth David   (R)

6100 Hefley Street   Tel. (714) 892-6623

Chabad House   (O)   *14401 Willow Lane   Tel. 596-1681*

Westwood

Adat Shalom   (C)

3030 Westwood Boulevard   Tel. (213) 475-4985

Chabad West Coast Headquarters   (O)

741 Gayley Avenue   Tel. 208-7511

Westwood Kehilla   (O)

900 Hilgard Avenue   Tel. 470-8343

Whittier 90604

Congregation Beth Shalom   (C)

14564 East Hawes Street   Tel. (213) 941-8744

Woodland Hills 91367

Beit Hamidrash of Woodland Hills   (O)

5850 Fallbrook Avenue   Tel. (818) 999-2059

Temple Aliyah (C)   *6025 Valley Circle   Tel. (818) 346-3545*
Temple Emet (R)   *20400 Ventura Boulevard   Tel. 348-0670*
Yorba Linda 92686
Chabad House (O)
                  19045 Yorba Linda Boulevard   Tel. (714) 693-0770
Yuba City 95992
Jewish Community Fellowship   (R)
                        P.O.Box 103   Tel. (916) 673-0561

MIKVEHS

Berkeley
Mikveh Taharas Israel
                  2520 Warring Street   Tel. (415) 848-7221
Long Beach
Mikveh Yisroel   *3847 Atlantic Avenue   Tel. (213) 427-1360*
Los Angeles
Los Angeles Mikveh
                  9548 West Pico Boulevard   Tel. (213) 550-4511
Mogen Abraham Synagogue
                  356 North La Brea Avenue   Tel. (213) 935-5415
Valley Mikveh Society
                  12800 Chandler Boulevard   Tel. (818) 506-0996
Oakland
Beth Jacob Congregation
                  3778 Park Boulevard   Tel. (415) 482-1147
San Francisco
Mikveh Israel B'nai David
                  3355 Sacramento Street   Tel. (415) 921-4070

OTHER SIGHTS

Angels Camp
OUTDOOR ADVENTURE RIVER SPECIALISTS
Tel. (209) 736-4677
Whitewater rafting outfitters. Fees start at $74 per day.

Auburn
GOLD COUNTRY MUSEUM
1273 High Street   Tel. (916) 889-4155

Barstow
CALICO GHOST TOWN
11 miles northeast of Barstow via I-15
There is a tour of an old silver mine, a museum and a train ride.

Calistoga
OLD FAITHFUL GEYSER
Located about 60 miles north of San Francisco one mile north on
Tubbs Lane between SR 29 and 128. It is one of the few regularly
erupting geysers in the world.
HOT AIR BALLOON RIDES
1458 Lincoln Avenue   Tel. (707) 942-6541
Tickets : Adults, $155
PETRIFIED FOREST
5 miles west on Petrified Forest Road   Tel. (707) 942-6667

Coloma
MARSHALL GOLD DISCOVERY HISTORIC PARK
Route 49   Tel. (916) 622-3470
In 1848, James Marshall discovered gold near John Sutter's sawmill.
This was the beginning of the California Gold Rush.

Columbia
COLUMBIA STATE HISTORIC PARK

Columbia was one of the largest and most important mining towns along the Mother Lode. Twelve square blocks in the old business district have been partially restored. There are stagecoach rides and you can pan for gold.

Danville
BEHRUNG AUTO MUSEUM

3750 Blackhawk Plaza Circle (East Bay area) Tel. (415) 736-2277
There are 70 distinctive automobiles on display, many worth over $1 million.

DEVIL'S POSTPILE NATIONAL MONUMENT

Located east of Yosemite National Park. Take US 395 to SR 203 to the Mammoth Mountain Ski Area parking lot. Then take a shuttle bus to the Postpile ranger station. The final leg of the trip is by a half-mile foot path.

The highlight of this 800-acre monument is a sheer wall of symmetrical basaltic columns more than 60 feet high. The formation is a remnant of a basalt lava flow worn smooth on top by glacial action.

There is a similar geologic formation in the Galil area of northern Israel. That formation is called *b'richat hameshushim,* which translates six-sided columns. After a lava flows cools very quickly it creates these elongated six-sided columns, similar to the Devils Postpile.

Downieville
GOLD PANNING

Route 49 (north of Grass Valley)
Old brick and stone buildings with picturesque iron doors and shutters flank the narrow, tree-lined main street. Some sections of sidewalk are still made of planks.
Gold panning is available downtown in the Yuba River.

Felton
ROARING CAMP & BIG TREES NARROW GAUGE RAILROAD
1 mile southeast on Graham Hill Road   Tel. (408) 335-4400
An 1880 steam train makes a 6-mile, 75-minute round trip as the conductor recounts the history of the Santa Cruz Mountains. Tickets: $10.95 for adults and $.95 for kids.

Fish Camp
YOSEMITE MOUNTAIN-SUGAR PINE RAILROAD
2 miles south on SR 41.   Tel. (209)683-7273
The scenic narrow-gauge railroad offers rides aboard gas-powered rail cars and a logger steam train.

Fort Bragg
CALIFORNIA WESTERN RAILROAD (The Skunk)
Pacific Coast Highway, SR 1   Tel. (707) 964-6371
The scenic 40-mile trip passes through redwood groves and crosses and recrosses the Noyo River.

Fortuna
CHAPMAN'S GEM & MINERAL MUSEUM
4 miles south off US 101   Tel. (707) 725-2495
There are displays of fossils, gems, minerals, petrified wood and Indian artifacts. (Donation)

San Juan Capistrano
MISSION SAN JUAN CAPISTRANO
2 blocks west of SR 74 / I-5 junction
This mission was founded in 1776. On every March 19 the swallows arrive.

Grass Valley
EMPIRE MINE STATE HISTORIC PARK
1 mile east of SR 49 at 10791 East Empire Street
Tel. (916) 273-8522

This mine produced nearly six million ounces of gold during its operation. The park has ten miles of hiking trails and a mine with 367 miles of passageways; restored buildings include the clubhouse, blacksmith shop, hoist house and machine shop.

Jamestown
RAILTOWN 1897 STATE HISTORIC PARK
Fifth Avenue   Tel. (209) 984-3953

GOLD PROSPECTING EXPEDITIONS
18170 Main Street (Livery Stable) Tel. (209) 984-4653
These outfitters have estimated that 4.2 million ounces of gold was mined last year. They will teach you the basic techniques: How to find the "Pay Streak" in streams; gold panning; sniping (locating gold nuggets in crevices); using a slice box; dredging; pocket hunting; location of tertiary placer deposits; electronic prospecting (metal detecting); and high-bank washing.
These outfitters also conduct whitewater rafting and helicopter trips.

Julian
EAGLE MINING COMPANY
North end of C Street   Tel. (619) 765-0036
There is a guided tour through a gold mine.

Lancaster
NASA AMES-DRYDEN FLIGHT RESEARCH FACILITY
25 miles northeast of SR 14 on Edwards Air Force Base
Tel. (805) 258-3446
This facility develops and tests new forms of aircraft design and flight operation techniques. There are tours of the facility which include a visit to a small aircraft and space museum. Reservations are highly recommended. (Free)

LASSEN VOLCANIC NATIONAL PARK
SR 36, nine miles east of Mineral.
This park is located in ancient and active volcanic region. There are several large and many small volcanoes, lava flows, hot springs, boiling lakes and mudpots. Note: It is highly recommended to stay on established trails at all times in hot springs or steaming areas. Ground crusts that appear safe can be dangerously thin!

LAVA BEDS NATIONAL MONUMENT
US 139, near the California-Oregon border   Tel. (916) 667-2282
The 46,500 acre area is characterized by cinder cones, deep chasms and nearly 200 lava tube caves of various sizes. Some of the caves contain permanent ice.

La Jolla
SAN DIEGO MUSEUM OF CONTEMPORARY ART
700 Prospect Street   Tel. (619) 454-3541
SCRIPP'S AQUARIUM-MUSEUM
8602 La Jolla Shores Drive   Tel. (619) 534-6933

Long Beach
LONG BEACH MUSEUM OF ART
2300 East Ocean Boulevard   Tel. (213) 439-2119
QUEEN MARY & SPRUCE GOOSE
Pier J, reached via Queen's Way Bridge or I-710
Tel. (213) 435-3511
The Queen Mary, one of the largest passenger liners ever built, is permanently moored at this pier in Long Beach Harbor.
The wooden flying boat Spruce Goose, designed by Howard Hughes, is the largest airplane ever built; its wingspan is 320 feet, and the fuselage is 219 feet long and constructed entirely from wood. Tickets: $17.50 for adults and $14 for kids.

Los Angeles

BRADBURY BUILDING
304 South Broadway   Tel. (213) 624-2378

EL PUEBLO DE LOS ANGELES HISTORIC PARK
Santa Ana Freeway (101) & Main Street   Tel. (213) 628-1274
Restoration of the original Los Angeles settlement. Visit the Pico
and Sepulveda Houses at 424 and 622 North Main Street.

CALIFORNIA MUSEUM OF SCIENCE AND INDUSTRY
700 State Drive   (Exposition Park)   Tel. (213) 744-7400

NATURAL HISTORY MUSEUM OF LOS ANGELES COUNTY
900 Exposition Boulevard   Tel. (213) 744-3466

LA BREA TAR PITS & PAGE MUSEUM
5801 Wilshire Boulevard   Tel. (213) 936-2230
These sticky asphalt beds trapped and preserved prehistoric plant
and animal life. The Page Museum displays the fossils and
reconstructed animals.

GENE AUTRY WESTERN HERITAGE MUSEUM
4700 Zoo Drive   (Griffith Park)   Tel. (213) 667-2000

GRIFFITH OBSERVATORY & PLANETARIUM
South Slope of Mount Hollywood (Griffith Park)
 Tel. (213) 664-1191

HERITAGE SQUARE MUSEUM
3800 Homer Street   Tel. (818) 449-0193

HOLLYHOCK HOUSE by FRANK LLOYD WRIGHT
4800 Hollywood Boulevard   Tel. (213) 662-7272
Located in Barnsdall Park, this is considered to be one of Frank
Lloyd Wright's finest works.

LOS ANGELES COUNTY MUSEUM OF ART
5905 Wilshire Boulevard   Tel. (213) 857-6111

LOS ANGELES MUNICIPAL ART GALLERY
4804 Hollywood Boulevard   Tel. (213) 660-4254

MUSEUM OF CONTEMPORARY ART
250 South Grand Avenue   Tel. (21`3)626-6222

THE MUSIC CENTER
First Street & Grand Avenue   Tel. (213) 972-7211

SOUTHWEST MUSEUM

234 Museum Drive   Tel. (213) 221-2163

STUDIO TOURS

KCET TV STUDIO TOUR

4401 Sunset Boulevard   Tel. (213) 667-9242

Tours Tuesday and Thursday mornings by reservation. (Free)

WATTS TOWER OF SIMON RODIA STATE HISTORIC PARK

1765 East 107th Street   Tel. (213) 569-8181

WELLS FARGO HISTORY MUSEUM

333 South Grand Avenue   Tel. (213) 253-7166

HOLLYWOOD STUDIO MUSEUM

East side of Highland Avenue, at the edge of the Hollywood Bowl
parking area.   Tel. (213) 874-2276

This is where Cecil B. DeMille, Jesse Lasky and Samuel Goldwyn
made their first feature film, *The Squaw Man*, in 1913. The museum
houses filmmaking exhibits, early camera equipment and a screening
room.

MANN'S CHINESE THEATRE

6925 Hollywood Boulevard

There are handprints and footprints of many past and present
movie stars imprinted in the concrete of the courtyard in front of
the theater.

NBC STUDIO TOUR

3000 West Alameda Avenue   (Burbank)   Tel. (818) 840-3537

A two-hour walking tour behind the scenes of a television
production studio. Free TV show tickets are available. Tour tickets:
$6.75 for adults, $5.75 for kids.

UNIVERSAL STUDIOS HOLLYWOOD

Hollywood Freeway (US 101)   (Burbank) Tel. (818) 508-9600

The entertainment center features a tram tour through Hollywood
stage sets, King Kong, Jaws, Earthquake and Pyscho. This is followed
by six live stage shows. Tickets: $24 for adults, $18.50 for kids.

WARNER BROTHERS STUDIOS V.I.P. TOUR

4000 Warner Boulevard   (Burbank)   Tel. (818) 954-1744

A very special behind-the-scenes tour of a movie and television studio, including live filming when possible. Reservations required one week in advance. Tickets: $22 (kids under 10 not admitted)

Malibu
J. PAUL GETTY MUSEUM
17985 Pacific Coast Highway   Tel. (213) 458-2300
Reservations required one week in advance.
MALIBU LAGOON MUSEUM
23200 Pacific Coast Highway   Tel. (213) 456-8432

Manteca
OAKWOOD LAKE WATER THEME PARK
874 East Woodward   Tel. (209) 239-9566
Take SR 120, between I-5 and SR 99 (near Stockton)

Mariposa
CALIFORNIA STATE MINING & MINERAL MUSEUM
(Near Yosemite National Park)   Tel. (209) 742-7625

Monterey
ALLEN KNIGHT MARITIME MUSEUM
550 Calle Principal   Tel. (408) 375-2553
COLTON HALL
Pacific Street   Tel. (408) 375-9944
MONTEREY BAY AQUARIUM
886 Cannery Row   Tel. (408) 648-4888
MONTEREY PENINSULA MUSEUM OF ART
559 Pacific Street   Tel. (408) 372-7591

Morgan Hill
WAGONS TO WINGS MUSEUM
15060 Foothill Road   Tel. (408) 779-4136

Mount Shasta
MOUNT SHASTA STATE FISH HATCHERY
1/2 mile west of I-5 via central Mount Shasta exit at Three, Old
State Road. Tel. (916) 926-2215

MUIR WOODS NATIONAL MONUMENT
17 miles northwest of San Francisco. Take Golden Gate Bridge and
SR 1. Tel. (415) 388-2595

Napa Valley
HOT AIR BALLOON RIDES
Tel. (415) 776-6382 $140 per person.

Nevada City
FIREHOUSE MUSEUM
214 Main Street   Tel. (916) 265-5468
MALKOFF DIGGINS STATE HISTORIC PARK
27 miles northeast off SR 49 on Tyler Foote Road.
 Tel. (916) 265-2740
This was the world's largest hydraulic gold mine.
THE MINERS FOUNDRY
325 Spring Street   Tel. (916) 265-5040

Newport Beach
NEWPORT HARBOR ART MUSEUM
850 San Clemente Drive   Tel. (714) 759-1122
SHERMAN LIBRARY & GARDENS
2647 East Coast Highway   Tel. (714) 673-2261

North Fork
SIERRA MONO INDIAN MUSEUM
Junction of CRs 225, 228, and 274.   Tel. (209) 877-2115

Novato
MARIN MUSEUM OF THE AMERICAN INDIAN
2200 Novato Boulevard   Tel. (415) 897-4064

Oakland
KAISER CENTER ART GALLERY
300 Lakeside Drive   Tel. (415) 271-2351
MORCOM AMPHITHEATER OF ROSES
700 Jean Street   Tel. (415) 658-0731
OAKLAND MUSEUM
10th & Oak Streets   Tel. (415) 273-3401

Pacific Grove
BUTTERFLY TREES
Ridge Road, off Lighthouse Avenue
Pine trees are covered with Monarch butterflies from late October
to March.
JOHN STEINBECK MEMORIAL MUSEUM
222 Central Avenue   Tel. (408) 373-6976
MUSEUM OF NATURAL HISTORY
165 Forest Avenue   Tel. (408) 372-4212

Palm Springs
MOORTEN BOTANICAL GARDEN
1701 South Palm Canyon Drive   Tel. (619)   327-6555
PALM SPRINGS AERIAL TRAMWAY
3 miles southwest of SR 111   Tel. (619) 325-1391
Rises to elevation of 8,516 fet above sea level. Tickets: $14.95
PALM SPRINGS DESERT MUSEUM
101 Museum Drive   Tel. (619) 325-7186

Palomar Mountain
PALOMAR OBSERVATORY
4.5 miles north on CR 56   Tel. (619) 742-2119

Paradise
GOLD NUGGET MUSEUM
502 Pearson Road   Tel. (916) 872-8722

Pasadena
THE GAMBLE HOUSE
4 Westmorland Place   Tel.   681-6427
NORTON SIMON MUSEUM
411 West Colorado Boulevard   Tel. (818) 449-3730
PACIFIC ASIA MUSEUM
46 North Los Robles Avenue   Tel. (818) 449-2742
TOURNAMENT HOUSE
391 South Orange Grove Boulevard   Tel. (818) 449-4100

Petaluma
CHEESE FACTORY
7500 Red Hill Road   Tel. (707) 762-6001
PETALUMA ADOBE STATE HISTORIC PARK
Adobe Road   Tel. (707) 762-4871
PETALUMA HISTORICAL LIBRARY & MUSEUM
20 4th Street   Tel. (707) 778-4398

Placerville
EL DORADO COUNTY HISTORICAL MUSEUM
100 Placerville Drive   Tel. (916) 621-5865

Randsburg
DESERT MUSEUM
161 Butte Avenue   Tel. (619) 374-2111

Redding
CARTER HOUSE NATURAL SCIENCE MUSEUM
48 Quartz Hill Road   Tel. (916) 225-4125
LAKE SHASTA CAVERNS
1.5 miles east of I-5 at O'Brien.   Tel. (916) 238-2341

REDDING MUSEUM
Caldwell Park   Tel. (916) 225-4155
SHASTA DAM
Tel. (916) 275-4463

Riverside
CALIFORNIA MUSEUM OF PHOTOGRAPHY
3824 Main Street   Tel. (714) 784-3686
JUROPA MOUNTAINS CULTURAL CENTER
7621 Granite Hill Drive   Tel. (714) 685-5818
MARCH FIELD MUSEUM
March Air Force Base   Tel. (714) 655-3725
Military aviation exhibits. Get pass at visitor center at the main gate.
RIVERSIDE MUNICIPAL MUSEUM
3720 Orange Street   Tel. (714) 782-5273
BOTANIC GARDENS at UNIVERSITY OF CALIFORNIA
North Campus Circle Drive, near parking lot 13   Tel. 787-4650

Sacramento
ACTION ADVENTURES WET N' WILD
Whitewater raft trips in nearby rivers.   Tel. (800) 238-3688
CALIFORNIA VEITNAM VETERANS MEMORIAL
15th & L Streets
CROCKER ART MUSEUM
216 O Street   Tel. (916) 449-5423
OLD GOVERNOR'S MANSION
16th & H Streets   Tel. (916) 445-4209
OLD SACRAMENTO
Capitol Mall, I Street, 2nd Street and the Sacramento River
Historic Gold Rush district with museums, restaurants and shops.
SACRAMENTO SCIENCE CENTER
3615 Auburn Boulevard   Tel. (916) 449-8256

STATE CAPITOL
10th, 15th, L and N Streets.   Tel. (916) 324-0333
Free guided tours are given.
SUTTER'S FORT
27th and L Streets   Tel. (916) 445-4209
TOWE FORD MUSEUM
Front Street at V Street   Tel. (916) 442-6802

San Andreas
CALAVERAS COUNTY HISTORICAL MUSEUM
30 North Main Street   Tel. (209) 754-6513
CALIFORNIA CAVERNS at CAVE CITY
8 miles east on Mountain Ranch Road   Tel. (209) 736-2708

San Diego
AEROSPACE HISTORICAL CENTER
Ford Building   (Balboa Park)   Tel. (619) 236-5717
HALL OF CHAMPIONS SPORTS MUSEUM
Balboa Park   Tel. (619) 234-2544
HOUSE OF PACIFIC RELATIONS
Balboa Park   Tel. (619) 234-0739
MUSEUM OF PHOTOGRAPHIC ARTS
Casa de Balboa   (Balboa Park)   Tel. (619) 239-5262
MUSEUM OF NATURAL HISTORY
El Prado   (Balboa Park)   Tel. (619) 232-3821
REUBEN H. FLEET SPACE THEATER
& SCIENCE CENTER
1875 El Prado   (Balboa Park)   Tel. (619) 238-1168
SAN DIEGO AUTOMOTIVE MUSEUM
Balboa Park   Tel. (619) 231-2886
SAN DIEGO MODEL RAILROAD MUSEUM
Casa de Balboa   (Balboa Park)   Tel. (619) 696-0199
SAN DIEGO MUSEUM OF ART
Balboa Park   Tel. (619) 232-7931

SAN DIEGO MUSEUM OF MAN
California Quadrangle   (Balboa Park)   Tel. (619) 239-2001
SAN DIEGO ZOO
Balboa Park   Tel.   234-3153
This is one of the largest zoos in the world. More than 3,200 animals are on display, separated from the public by moats.. The zoo is landscaped with tropical and subtropical vegetation. Moving sidewalks stretch from deep canyon to upper levels and an aerial tramway runs from the main entrance to the Horn and Hoof Mesa. Tickets: Adults, $10.75 and $4 for kids
SEA WORLD
Mission Bay's south shore   Tel. (619) 939-6212
SAN DIEGO UNION MUSEUM
2626 San Diego Avenue
This newspaper was founded in 1868.
SEELEY STABLES
2648 Calhoun Street
Collection of horse-drawn vehicles includes covered wagons and stagecoaches.
WHALEY HOUSE
2482 San Diego Avenue   Tel. (619) 298-2482
MARITIME MUSEUM OF SAN DIEGO
Embarcadero - 1306 North Harbor Drive   Tel. (619) 234-9153
SEAPORT VILLAGE
Ketner Boulevard   Tel. (619) 235-4014
FIREHOUSE MUSEUM
1572 Columbia Street   Tel. (619) 232-3473

San Francisco
ALCATRAZ ISLAND   Tel. (415) 546-2896
Former maximum security Federal penitentiary in San Francisco Bay where such notorious criminals as Al Capone, Machine Gun Kelly and Robert Stroud, the "Birdman of Alcatraz," were interned. Tickets at Fisherman's Wharf - Pier 41.

ANSEL ADAMS CENTER
250 4th Street   Tel. (415) 495-7000
ASIAN ART MUSEUM
Golden Gate Park   Tel. (415) 668-8921
CALIFORNIA ACADEMY OF SCIENCES
Golden Gate Park   Tel. (415) 750-7145
Includes the Natural History Museum, Steinhart Aquarium and Morrison Planetarium.

CALIFORNIA PALACE OF THE LEGION OF HONOR
Lincoln Park   Tel. (415) 750-3659
Displays includes works by Rembrandt, Rubens, Goya, El Greco, Manet, Monet, Renoir, Cezanne and Rodin.
CHINATOWN
Grant Avenue & Bush Street

DE YOUNG MEMORIAL MUSEUM
Golden Gate Park - Teagarden Drive   Tel. (415) 750-3659
CROOKEDEST STREET IN THE WORLD
Lombard Street, between Hyde and Leavenworth Streets.
40-degree slope in a series of hair-pin S-curves.
GOLDEN GATE BRIDGE
Vehicular US 101 and pedestrian walkway spans 8,981 feet over San Francisco Bay.
GOLDEN GATE PARK
Conservatory of Flowers - Kennedy Drive
Japanese Tea Garden
Strybing Arboretum - 9th Avenue
GUINNESS MUSEUM OF WORLD RECORDS
235 Jefferson Street   Tel. (415) 771-9890
OLD U.S. MINT
Fifth & Mission Streets   Tel. (415) 744-6830
Opened in 1874 to serve the rich mineral districts of the California Gold Rush. It survived the 1906 earthquake. Exhibits of gold bars, medals, coinage and mining artifacts.

PALACE OF FINE ARTS
Baker Street & Marina Boulevard
Last remaining structure of the 1915 Panama-Pacific Exposition.
RIPLEY'S BELIEVE IT OR NOT MUSEUM
Fisherman's Wharf   Tel. (415) 771-6188
SAN FRANCISCO ART MUSEUM
800 Chestnut Street   Tel. (415) 771-7020
SAN FRANCISCO EXPERIENCE
Fisherman's Wharf - Pier 39   Tel. (415) 982-7550
SAN FRANCISCO FIRE DEPARTMENT MUSEUM
655 Presidio Avenue   Tel. (415) 861-8000
WAX MUSEUM
145 Jefferson Street   Tel. (415) 885-4975
WELLS FARGO HISTORY MUSEUM
420 Montgomery Street   Tel. (415) 396-2619
Contains a stagecoach, relics of the Gold Rush and nuggets.
WORLD OF ECONOMICS
Federal Reserve Bank - 101 Market Street   Tel. (415) 974-3252
Exhibits on economy and banking operations with electronic
interactive devices and computer games.

San Simeon
HEARST CASTLE & ESTATE
Along SR 1 (Pacific Coastal Highway) Tel. (805) 927-2020
William Randolph Hearst, the newspaper tycoon, built this lavish
estate in 1919. It was designed by a woman architect, Julia Morgan.
The main residence is a huge Hispano-Moorish building where
millions of dollars' worth of Hearst art collection and antiques are
displayed. Pools, fountains and statuary adorn the landscaped
gardens. There are four individual tours, each costing $12.

YOSEMITE NATIONAL PARK
Tel. (209) 372-0200

KID STUFF

Anaheim
DISNEYLAND
1313 Harbor Boulevard (I-5)   Tel. (714) 999-4565

The original Disneyland is located just south of Los Angeles. There are six theme areas: Tomorrowland, Frontierland, Fantasyland, Adventureland, Critter Country and New Orleans Square.

Passports covers admission to the park and all rides and attractions: $25.50 for adults, $20.50 for kids.

HOBBY CITY DOLL & TOY MUSEUM
1238 South Beach Boulevard   Tel. (714) 527-2323

This museum contains over 3,000 dolls and toys housed in a half-scale model of the White House.

Buena Park
KNOTT'S BERRY FARM
8039 Beach Boulevard   Tel. (714) 220-5200

Located near Disneyland, Knott's Berry Farm recreates the atmosphere of the Old West and encompasses five theme areas. Tickets: Adults, $21 and $17 for kids.

MEDIEVAL TIMES
7662 Beach Boulevard   Tel. (714) 521-4740

Renaissence festivities performed by costumed knights. Tickets: $26.95+ for adults and $18.95 for kids.

MOVIELAND WAX MUSEUM
7711 Beach Boulevard   Tel. (714) 522-1154

Fairfield
SCANDIA FAMILY FUN CENTER
I-80 (northeast of San Francisco) to Suisun Valley Road
Tel. (707) 864-8338

Miniature golf, waterbug bumper boats, Little Indy race cars and a train ride.

WESTERN RAILWAY MUSEUM
12 miles east on SR 12   Tel. (707) 374-2978
Exhibits of vintage street cars, a Blackpool English open tram, a New York City "El", and streetcar rides.
Tickets: $10 for adults and $8 for kids. (Closed November-February)

Irvine
WILD RIVERS WATERPARK
8800 Irvine Center Drive   Tel. (714) 768-9453
This park encompasses 20 acres devoted to more than 40 water rides and attractions. Tickets: $14.95 for adults and $10.95 for kids.

Lake Tahoe
PONDEROSA RANCH
SR 28 in Incline Village (Nevada)   Tel. (702) 831-0691
This is a western theme park featuring the original Cartwright ranch house from the television show "Bonanza." There is a saloon, museum, kiddyland, playground, petting farm and mystery mine.
Tickets: Adults, $8.50 and kids, $7.50.

Long Beach
LONG BEACH CHILDREN'S MUSEUM
445 Long Beach Boulevard   Tel. (213-495-11643

Los Angeles
LOS ANGELES CHILDREN'S MUSEUM
310 North Main Street   Tel. (213) 612-3320
LOS ANGELES ZOO
Junction Golden State & Ventura Freeways   Tel. (213) 666-4090

Monterey
DENNIS THE MENACE PLAYGROUND
El Estero   Tel. (408) 646-3866

Newport Beach
NEWPORT DUNES AQUATIC PARK
Pacific Coast Highway at Jamboree Road   Tel. (714) 644-0510

Oakdale
HERSHEY CHOCOLATE, U.S.A.
1400 South Yosemite Avenue   Tel. (209) 847-0381

Oakland
CHILDREN'S FAIRYLAND
Grand Avenue (Lakeside Park)   Tel. (415) 832-3609
OAKLAND ZOO at KOWLAND PARK
98th Avenue at I-580   Tel. (415) 632-9523

Palm Springs
OASIS WATERPARK
1500 Gene Autry Trail   Tel. (619) 325-7873
Tickets: Adults, $14.50 and $9.95 for kids

Pasadena
KIDSPACE
390 South El Molino Avenue   Tel. (818) 449-9143
Hands-on exhibits that include a TV studio, radio station and
"grown-up" tools.

Petaluma
WINNERS CIRCLE RANCH
5911 Lakeville Highway   Tel. (707) 762-1808
Miniature horses , horse shows, wagon rides.

Piercy
CONFUSION HILL
Us 101 Tel. (707) 925-6456
Miniature train ride through redwood forest and tree tunnel.

WORLD FAMOUS TREE HOUSE
5 miles south on US 101   Tel. (707) 925-6406
4,000-year-old living tree, 250 feet high and 33 feet in diameter.

Pleasanton
RAPIDS WATERSLIDE at
SHADOW CLIFFS REGIONAL RECREATION AREA
2 miles east on Stanley Boulevard   Tel. (415) 829-6230

Port Costa
MURIEL'S DOLL HOUSE MUSEUM
33 Canyon Lake Drive   Tel. (415) 787-2820

Redding
WATERWORKS PARK
151 North Boulder Drive   Tel. (916) 246-9550

Sacramento
FAIRYTALE TOWN
William Land Park   Tel. (916) 449-5233
SACRAMENTO ZOO
Land Park Drive   Tel. (916) 449-5885
WATERWORLD USA
1600 Exposition Boulevard   Tel. (916) 924-0555

San Francisco
EXPOLRATORIUM
Bay & Lyon Streets   Tel (415)561-0360
Hands-on exhibits explore science, math, technology and animal behavior.
SAN FRANCISCO ZOO
Sloat Boulevard at 45th Avenue   Tel. (415)753-7083

San Jose
CHILDREN'S DISCOVERY MUSEUM
Woz Way & Auzerais Street   Tel. (408) 298-5495
HAPPY HOLLOW
Kelley Park - 1300 Senter Road   Tel. (408) 292-8188
RAGING WATERS
Lake Cunnungham Regional Park
Capitol Expressway at Tully Road   Tel. (408) 238-9900

Santa Clarita
SIX FLAGS MAGIC MOUNTAIN
I-% at 26101 Magic Mountain Parkway   Tel. (805) 255-4111
260-acre entertainment complex with more than 100 rides, shows
and attractions. See diving and dolphin shows and the Tidal Wave,
which plunges over a 50-foot waterfall. Tickets: Adults - $23;
children under 48" - $11.

Vacaville (Napa Valley)
WOOZ FAMILY AMUSEMENT PARK
500 Orange Drive near I-80 at I-505   Tel. (707) 446-3977
Participants race against the clock to finish the obstacle course.

COLORADO

There is no definite record as to when the first Jews came to Colorado. It is known, however, that they arrived around the time of the Civil War, and many years prior to Colorado's admission to the Union and statehood. In the 1870s, a large community already existed in Leadville, sufficiently numerous and prosperous to possess a synagogue. In the early days, there were also smaller settlements in Denver, Central City, Cotopaxi, Pueblo, Trinidad, Cripple Creek, Boulder, Colorado City (Springs), Silverton, and other mining camps.

It is well known that the little town of Leadville was the birthplace of one of the greatest fortunes of all times - that of the Guggenheim family. No others did as well, and most had very little to show for their years of struggling in the new frontiers.

It is noteworthy that there should have been any Jewish pioneers at all in those days. Frontier followers have always been a burly lot, particularly in the early mining-camp days in the the west. Mere existence was a bitter struggle, for there were many hardships to be overcome, and actual physical dangers were great. Mining men were notoriously devoid of sympathy, compassion and tolerance, particularly toward those who differed from themselves in religious beliefs. Consider, then, the tremendous courage and fortitude of those early Jewish pioneers who settled here, despite these obstacles. Most were newly-arrived immigrants who barely spoke or understood the English language.Many persisted in the observance of religious customs, which seemed strange to their neighbors, and automatically subjected these immigrants to much ridicule.

As gold, silver, and lead strikes began dotting Colorado with mining camps in the 1860s and 1870s, Jewish entrepreneurs established stores, wholesale houses, banks, theaters, freighting companies, stagecoach lines, and even saloons in the towns. In the frontier communities most of them destined to become ghost towns, the Jewish businessmen were almost always aligned with the sober, law-abiding forces and were regarded as solid citizens.

The oldest existing Jewish organization in the state, the Denver B'nai B'rith Lodge, was founded in 1872 by Louis Anfenger, who arrived in Colorado in the late 1860s. In 1874, B'nai B'rith and the Hebrew Burial and Prayer Society joined forces to establish Temple Emanu-El, Colorado's first permanent Jewish congregation with 21 members. Temple Emanu-El's earliest house of worship was dedicated in 1876, the year Colorado was admitted to the Union. In 1879, the Beth Hamedrash Hagadol was founded under the leadership of Henry Plonsky as the first East European congregation. That year a YMHA was formed. By 1882 Denver boasted of seven Jewish congregations.

Until 1880 most of the Jews who settled in Colorado were of German origin, but thereafter the bulk of newcomers came from East Europe. Most of the 60 families who had been settled by the Jewish Agricultural Society at Atwood and Cotopaxi, two ill-fated agricultural colonies, ultimately found their way to Denver where they became the nucleus of the early Orthodox Jewish community of Russian Jews.

Along with the gold-seekers came the health-seekers. The air and sunshine of Denver, also known as the "Mile-High-City," was the popular prescription for tuberculosis. Francis Wisebart Jacobs, wife of Abraham Jacobs, a city councilman and civic leader, was one of the organizers of the National Jewish Hospital. Her portrait appears in a stained-glass window in rotunda of the State Capitol.

There are approximately 30,000 Jews in Denver. There are also small settlements in the ski resort towns of Aspen, Evergreen and Vail.

Colorado Springs

OLD JEWISH CEMETERY

Colorado Springs was originally called Colorado City. The Hebrew Benevolent Society was founded in 1898 and a Jewish cemetery acquired in 1901. It is located on South Hancock Road and is now part of the city-owned Evergreen Cemetery.

Temple Shalom, located at 1523 East Monument, is a merger of former Congregation B'nai Israel and Temple Beth El.

U.S. AIR FORCE ACADEMY CADET CHAPEL

This soaring structure of glass, steel and aluminum houses separate Jewish, Catholic and Protestant chapels. The Jewish chapel is the first specifically-designed Jewish place of worship built on a U.S. military installation.

Denver

ANFENGER HOUSE
2900 Champa Street

This stately old house built in 1884 by Louis Anfenger, one of the pioneer Jews in Denver, is part of a designated historic district.

BABI YAR PARK
South Parker Road at Havanah

This was the world's first memorial to the thousands of Jews massacred by the Nazis near Kiev, Russia, September 29-30, 1941.

CARMIEL PARK

Denver's sister city is Carmiel, Israel. The park is located on the north bank of Cherry Creek, from Steele Street to the City of Takayuma Park. The park was dedicated in 1979.

COLORADO HALL OF FAME

There is a stained-glass window portrait of Frances Wisebart Jacobs, who was one of the founders of the National Jewish Hospital. There is also a portrait of Otto Mears who built the Rio Grande Southern (1890-1892); the Silverton (1887); and the Silverton Northern Railroads. The portraits are located in the rotunda of the State Capitol.

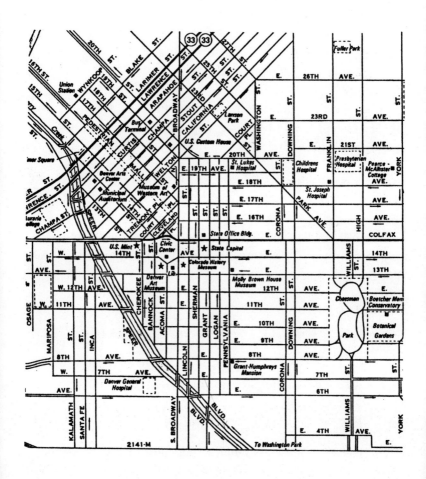

DENVER

CONGREGATION ZERA ABRAHAM
1560 Winona Court   Tel. (303) 825-7517

This congregation was founded by the Russian Jewish immigrants of the Cotopaxi colony who moved to Denver after the colony failed.

EMMANUEL GALLERY
Lawrence & 10th Streets

This fieldstone building was designed as the Emmanuel Episcopal Church. It was sold to Congregation Shearith Israel in 1903. It was known as the "10th Street Shul. "Today, the building is an historic landmark and is used as a student information center and art gallery. The memorial tablets that once hung in the synagogue are now located in Congregation Rodef Shalom.

NATIONAL JEWISH HOSPITAL & RESEARCH CENTER
3800 East Colfax Avenue

This internationally-known, free, non-sectarian medical center for chest diseases, is the oldest of Denver's three national health institutions. It was organized by Mrs. Frances Wisebart Jacobs with the help of the noted Rabbi William Friedman of Temple Emanuel. The hospital was built in 1893.

OLDEST SYNAGOGUE IN COLORADO
Temple Emanuel
51 Grape Street   Tel. (303) 388-4013

This is the oldest existing congregation in Colorado. It was founded in 1874. Its noted rabbi, William S. Friedman, held that position from 1900 to 1939. The former synagogue building, located at 16th and Pearl Streets, was designed in Moorish-Revival style in 1899 by John Humphrey. The building features two towers 150 feet high and capped with copper minarets. That building is still extant and is used as an Events Center.

The congregation's present building was designed by Percival Goodman in 1956. Temple Emanuel follows the Reform ritual.

THE CRYING ROOM
Hebrew Educational Alliance
1555 Stuart Street   Tel. (303) 629-0410

The architects of this Orthodox congregation designed a special space in this synagogue. At one time there was something called a "shabbos microphone," which permitted this special electronic device to be used on the Sabbath.

During the rabbi's sermon or during the reading of the Torah, if a child would disturb the services by crying, the mother would take the child to a small glass-enclosed room in the back of the main sanctuary. This room would have the services "piped-in" via the microphone. The mother could hear and see the services from this "Crying Room" and not disturb the rest of the congregation.

MIZEL MUSEUM OF JUDAICA
Beth Hamedrash Hagadol
560 South Monaco Parkway   Tel. (303) 333-4156

Denver's Temple Emanuel, former building.

This museum contains changing exhibits on international and local Jewish subjects. There are tours, lectures and films available. The museum hours are Monday-Thursday 10-4 and Sunday 10-noon.

Leadville

DAVID MAY MEMORIAL
318 Harrison Avenue

This large boulder with a metal plaque marks the site where David May established his clothing store in a tent in 1877 during the silver boom.

TEMPLE ISRAEL (FORMER)
Pine & West 4th Streets

This was the location of Temple Israel, when Leadville was once a flourishing Jewish community.

Trinidad

CONGREGATION AARON
305 Maple Street   Tel. (303) 846-2685

This is the second oldest congregation in Colorado. It was founded in 1878 and occupies a synagogue building erected in 1889. The congregation follows the Reform ritual.

KOSHER PROVISIONS

Denver

B & J Utica Grocery
  4500 West Colfax Avenue   Tel. 534-2253

The Bagel Store
  942 South Monaco Parkway   Tel. 388-2648

Oroweat and Star Bakery Products
  5050 East Evans Avenue   Tel. 758-1915

Boscoe's Variety Breads
  240 Bryant   Tel. 934-2901

East Side Kosher Deli
  5600 East Cedar Avenue   Tel. 322-9862

Kosher Connection Caterers
  6495 East Virginia   Tel. 355-3723

Mediterranean Health Cafe
  2817 East 3rd Avenue   Tel. (303) 399-2940

Meyers Kosher Meat Market
  3211 East Colfax Avenue   Tel. 377-2729

Singers Gourmet Catering
  303 South Jasmine   Tel. 355-4293

Steinberg's Kosher Grocery
  4017 West Colfax Avenue   Tel. 534-0314

SYNAGOGUES

Adams   80209
Allied Jewish Chapel
>   *Allied Apartments   22 South Adams Street*

Arvada   80005
Congregation B'nai Torah - Northwest Jewish Community
>   *P.O.Box 5488   Tel. 469-0750*

Aspen   81611
Aspen Jewish Center
>   *0077 Meadowood Drive   Tel. 925-8245*

Aurora   80115
Aurora Community Synagogue - Adat Shalom   (R)
>   *1092 South Nome Street   Tel. 690-4108*

Boulder   80303
Congregation Bonai Shalom   (C)
>   *1527 Cherryvale Street   Tel. (303) 442-6605*
Chabad House   (O)   *3100 Arapahoe   Tel. 440-7772*
Congregation Har Hashem   (R)
>   *3950 Baseline Road   Tel. 499-7077*

Colorado Springs   80909
Chabad House   (O)
>   *3465 Nonchalant Circle East   Tel. (719) 596-7330*
Temple Shalom   (C/R)
>   *1523 East Monument Street   Tel. 634-5311*
U.S. Air Force Academy - Cadet Chapel   (R)   80840
>   Fort Carson Military Reservation   *Tel. (719) 472-2636*

Denver   80224
Beth Hamedrash Hagadol Congregation   (O)
>   *560 South Monaco Parkway   Tel. (303) 388-4203*
Beth Joseph Congregation   (T)
>   *825 Ivanhoe Street   Tel. 355-7321*

Chabad House   (O)   *400 South Holly Street   Tel. 329-0211*
Colorado Reconstructionist Federation   (Rec)
                         6445 East Ohio   Tel. 388-4441
East Denver Orthodox Synagogue   (O)
                   198 South Holly Street Tel. 322-7943
Temple Emanu-El   (R)   *51 Grape Street   Tel. 388-4013*
Hebrew Educational Alliance   (O)
                   1555 Stuart Street   Tel. 629-0410
Kohlet Chavurah   (T)
                   6001 East 9th Avenue   Tel. 388-4211
Temple Micah   (R)   *2600 Leyden Street   Tel. 388-4239*
Ostrover Beth Jacob Congregation   (T)
                Beth Israel Home and Hospital
                   1601 Lowell Boulevard   Tel. 825-2190
Congregation Rodef Shalom   (C)
                   450 South Kearney Street   Tel. 399-0035
Temple Sinai   (R)   *3509 South Glencoe Street   Tel. 759-1827*
Southeast Synagogue   (C)
                   6984 East Jarvis Place   Tel. 759-4019
Talmudic Research Institute   (O)
                   4634 West 14th Avenue   Tel. 623-8466
Yeshiva Toras Chaim   (O)
                   1400 Quitman Street   Tel. 629-8200
Tri-Sulom Congregation   (Chassidic)   Kehillas Yaakov   (O)
                   295 South Locust Street   Tel. 377-1200
Congregation Zera Abraham   (O)
                   1560 Winona Court   Tel. 825-7517
Congregation Zera Israel   (Lit'visha Shul)   (O)
                   3934 West 14th Avenue   Tel. 571-0166
Durango   81301
Four Corners Jewish Community Center
                   101 West 9th Street   Tel. 259-2971
Evergreen 80439
Congregation Beth Evergreen   *P.O.Box 415 Tel. 1-838-6419*

Fort Collins 80524

Chabad House   (O)

904 East Elizabeth Street   Tel. (303) 484-9971

Congregation Har Shalom

P.O.Box 12   (80522)   Tel. 223-5191

Grand Junction 81501

Congregation Ohr Shalom

441 Kennedy Avenue   Tel. 243-2491

Greeley 80631

Beth Israel Congregation

1625 Reservoir Road   P.O.Box 867   Tel. 353-0869

Littleton 80121

Congregation Beth Shalom   (C)

2280 East Noble Place   Tel. (303) 794-6643

Loveland 80539

Northern Colorado Jewish Center

P.O.Box 2133   Tel. (303) 226-0940

Pueblo 81003

Temple Emanu-El   (R)

1325 North Grand Avenue   Tel. (303) 544-6448

United Hebrew Center   (C)

106 West 15th Street   Tel. 544-9897

Steamboat Springs 80477

Congregation Har Mishpachat

P.O.Box 770307   Tel. (303) 879-0064

Trinidad 81082

Congregation Aaron   (R)

305 Maple Street   Tel. (303) 846-2685

Vail 81658

B'nai Vail Congregation

Vail Interfaith Chapel   *Tel. 476-1955*

MIKVEH

Denver 80204

Jewish Women's League of Denver

1404 Quitman Street   Tel. (303) 893-5315

OTHER SIGHTS

Arriba
TARADO MANSION (1917)
Exit 383 on I-70   Tel. (719) 768-3468

Aspen
GHOST TOWNS
Ashcroft - 12 miles south on Castle Creek Road
Independence - 15 miles east on US 82
STALLARD HOUSE MUSEUM
620 West Bleeker Street   Tel. (303) 925-3721

Boulder
BOULDER HISTORICAL MUSEUM
1206 Euclid Avenue
NATIONAL CENTER FOR ATMOSPHERIC RESEARCH
1850 Table Mesa Drive   Tel. (303) 497-1174
UNIVERSITY OF COLORADO MUSEUM
Broadway & 15th Street   Tel. (303) 492-6892

Canon City
BUCKSKIN JOE (Log Cabins)
Royal Gorge Road   Tel. (719) 275-5149
CANON CITY MUNICIPAL MUSEUM
6th & Royal Gorge Boulevard   Tel. (719) 269-9018
ESTES INDUSTRIES (Model rocket ships)
Tel. (719) 372-6565

Central City
NARROW GAUGE RAILROAD
220 Spring Street   Tel. (303) 433-7872
GILPIN COUNTY MUSEUM
Eureka Street   Tel. (303) 582-5283

THE OPERA HOUSE   (1878)
Eureka Street   Tel. (303) 582-5202
TELLER HOUSE   (1872)
Tel. (303) 582-3200
THOMAS-BILLINGS HOME   (1874)
209 Eureka Street   Tel. (303) 582-5093

COLORADO NATIONAL MONUMENT
US 340   Tel. (303) 858-3617

Colorado Springs
BEAR CREEK NATURE CENTER
245 Bear Creek Road (26th Street)   Tel. 633-9218
COLORADO SPRINGS PIONEER MUSEUM
215 South Tejon Street   Tel. 578-6650
EL POMAR CARRIAGE HOUSE MUSEUM
Lake Avenue   Tel. 634-7711
FINE ARTS CENTER
30 West Dale Street   Tel. 634-5581
MAY NATURAL HISTORY MUSEUM
Nevada Avenue   Tel. 576-0450
McALLISTER HOUSE   (1873)
423 North Cascade Avenue   Tel. 635-7925
MUSEUM OF THE AMERICAN NUMISMATIC ASSOC.
818 North Cascade Avenue   Tel. 632-2646
NATIONAL CARVERS MUSEUM
Cheyenne Boulevard & High Drive   Tel. 481-2656
PETERSON SPACE COMMAND MUSEUM
4 miles east on US 24   Tel. 554-4915
PIKES PEAK GHOST TOWN
400 South 21st Street   Tel. 634-0691
PRORODEO HALL OF FAME
101 Pro Rodeo Drive   Tel. 593-8840
U.S. AIR FORCE ACADEMY
12 miles north on I-25   Tel. 472-2025

VAN BRIGGLE ART POTTERY
600 South 21st Street   Tel. 633-4080
WESTERN MUSEUM OF MINING & INDUSTRY
1025 North Gate Road   Tel. 598-8850
WHITE HOUSE RANCH LIVING HISTORY SITE
Gateway Road   Tel. 578-6777
WORLD FIGURE SKATING HALL OF FAME
20 First Street   Tel. 635-5200

Craig
MOFFAT COUNTY MUSEUM
221 West Victory Way   Tel. (303) 824-6360

Cripple Creek
CRIPPLE CREEK DISTRICT MUSEUM
Bennett Avenue   Tel. (719) 689-2634
MOLLIE KATHLEEN GOLD MINE (Tour)
Cripple Creek & US 67   Tel. (719) 689-2465

Delta
DELTA COUNTY MUSEUM
5th & Palmer Streets   Tel. (303) 874-3791

Denver
DENVER MUSEUM OF NATURAL HISTORY
City Park   Tel. (303) 322-7009
DENVER ART MUSEUM
100 West 14th Street
COLORADO HISTORY MUSEUM
13th & Broadway   Tel. (303) 866-3682
DENVER ARTS CENTER
Curtis & 14th Streets   Tel. (303) 893-DCPA
DENVER BOTANIC GARDENS
1005 York Street   Tel. (303) 331-4000
ELITCH GARDENS
38th Avenue & Tennyson Street   Tel. (303) 455-4771

FORNEY TRANSPORTATION MUSEUM
1416 Platte Street   Tel. (303) 433-3643
GRANT HUMPHREYS MANSION   (1882)
770 Pennsylvania Street   Tel. (303) 866-3507
MOLLY BROWN HOUSE MUSEUM   (1889)
1340 Pennsylvania Street   Tel. (303) 832-4092
MUSEUM OF WESTERN ART
1727 Tremont Place   Tel. (303) 296-1880
DENVER MUSEUM OF MINIATURES, DOLLS & TOYS
1880 Gaylord   Tel. (303) 322-3704
TRIANON MUSEUM & ART GALLERY
335 14th Street   Tel. (303) 623-0739
U.S. MINT
300 West Colfax Avenue   Tel. (303) 844-3582

Dolores
ANASAZI HERITAGE CENTER
US 184   Tel. (303) 882-4811

Durango
THE SILVERTON NARROW GAUGE RAILROAD
Durango-Silverton   Tel. (303) 247-2733

Estes Park
AERIAL TRAMWAY
Tel. (303) 586-3675
ESTES PARK ADVENTURES (Rafting trips)
Tel. (303) 586-2303

ESTES PARK AREA HISTORIC MUSEUM
200 4th Street   Tel. (303) 586-6256
MacGREGOR RANCH & MUSEUM
US 34   Tel. (303) 586-3749
**RICKER-BARTLETT PEWTER CASTING STUDIO
& GALLERY**
2 miles east on US 34   Tel. (303) 586-2030

Golden
ADOLPH COORS CO. (Brewery tours)
13 & Ford Streets   Tel. (303) 277-BEER
ASTOR HOUSE HOTEL MUSEUM   (1867)
822 12th Street   Tel. (303) 278-3557
COLORADO RAILROAD MUSEUM
17155 West 44th Avenue   Tel. (303) 279-4591
COLORADO SCHOOL OF MINES GEOLOGY MUSEUM
16th & Maple Streets   Tel. (303) 273-3823
HERITAGE SQUARE
US 40   Tel. (303) 277-0040
PIONEER MUSEUM
911 10th Street

Grand Junction
DINOSAUR VALLEY
4th & Main Streets   Tel. ((303) 243-3466
MUSEUM OF WESTERN COLORADO
4th & Ute Avenues   Tel. (303) 242-0971

GREAT SAND DUNES NATIONAL MONUMENT
Tel. (719) 378-2312

Greeley
CENTENNIAL VILLAGE
1475 A Street   Tel. (303) 353-6123
MEEKER MUSEUM
1324 9th Avenue   Tel. (303) 353-6123

Gunnison
PIONEER MUSEUM
US 50   Tel. (303) 641-1501
Gunnison National Monument
BLACK CANYON
Tel. (303) 249-7036

Hot Sulphur Springs
GRAND COUNTY MUSEUM
US 40   Tel. (303) 725-3939

Idaho Springs
ARGO GOLD MILL
2350 Riverside Drive   Tel. (303) 567-2421
EDGAR MINE
Colorado Avenue & 8th Street   Tel. (303) 273-3701

Leadville
EARLY LEADVILLE (Film)
809 Harrison Avenue
H.A.W. TABOR HOME   (1881)
116 East 5th Street   Tel. (719) 486-0551
HEALY HOUSE   (1878)
912 Harrison Avenue   Tel. (719) 486-0487
HERITAGE MUSEUM
9th Street & Harrison Avenue   Tel. (719) 486-1878
LEADVILLE, COLORADO & SOUTHERN RAILROAD
US 24   Tel. (719) 486-3936
THE MATCHLESS MINE CABIN
East 7th Street   Tel. (719) 486-0371
THE NATIONAL MINING HALL OF FAME
120 West 9th   Tel. (719) 486-1229
TABOR OPERA HOUSE   (1879)
US 24 & 4th Street   Tel. (719) 486-1147

Limon
LIMON TWILIGHT LIMITED TRAIN RIDES
I-70   Tel. (719) 775-2819

Littleton
LITTLETON HISTORICAL MUSEUM
6028 South Gallup   Tel. (303) 795-3850

Longmont
LONGMONT MUSEUM
375 Kimbark   Tel. (303) 776-6050

Loveland
ANTIQUE AUTO HOUSE
3312 North Garfield   Tel. (303) 667-7040
LOVELAND MUSEUM & GALLERY
503 Lincoln Avenue   Tel. (303) 667-6070

Lyons
LYONS REDSTONE MUSEUM
338 High Street   Tel. (303) 823-6692

Manitou Springs
BUFFALO BILL WAX MUSEUM
404 West Manitou Avenue   Tel. (719) 685-5900
CAVE OF THE WINDS
US 24   Tel. (719) 685-5444
MANITOU CLIFF DWELLINGS MUSEUM
US 24   Tel. (719) 685-5242
MIRAMONT CASTLE   (1895)
9 Capitol Hill Avenue   Tel. (719) 685-1011
MOUNT MANITOU SCENIC RAILWAY
515 Ruxton Avenue   Tel. (719) 685-9086
PIKES PEAK COG RAILWAY
515 Ruxton Avenue   Tel. (719) 685-5401

Meeker
WHITE RIVER MUSEUM
US 13   Tel. (303) 878-9982

MESA VERDE NATIONAL PARK
Tel. (303) 533-7731

Silverton
SAN JUAN COUNTY MUSEUM
Green Street   Tel. (303) 387-5838

Steamboat Springs
TREAD OF PIONEER MUSEUM
5th & Oak Streets   Tel. (303) 879-2214

Sterling
OVERLAND TRAIL MUSEUM
US 6 & Platte River Bridge   Tel. (303) 522-3895

Strassburg
COMANCHE CROSSING & MUSEUM
Tel. (303) 622-4668

Telluride
SAN MIGUEL COUNTY HISTORICAL MUSEUM
317 North Fir Street   Tel. (303) 728-3344

Trinidad
A.R.MITCHELL MEMORIAL MUSEUM
131 West Main Street   Tel. (719) 846-4224
BACA HOUSE & PIONEER MUSEUM
Main Street   Tel. (719) 846-7217
BLOOM HOUSE   (1882)
300 East Main Street   Tel. (719) 846-7217

Vail
VAIL SKI MUSEUM
I-70   Tel. (303) 476-1876

HAWAII

SYNAGOGUES

Honolulu 96817
Chabad House   (O)
                          4851 Kahala Avenue   Tel. (808) 735-8161
Temple Emanu-El   (R)   *2550 Pali Highway   Tel. 595-7521*
Pearl Harbor   96860
Aloha Jewish Chapel   (R)
                    Pearl Harbor Naval Station   Tel. (808) 471-0050

Honolulu's Temple Emanu-El.

OTHER SIGHTS

ISLAND OF HAWAII

HAWAII VOLCANOES NATIONAL PARK
Tel. (808) 967-7643

Hilio
AKAKA FALLS STATE PARK
HAWAII TROPICAL BOTANICAL GARDEN
Tel. (808) 964-5233
KAUMANA CAVES
Saddle Road
LYMAN MISSION HOUSE & MUSEUM
276 Haili Street   Tel. (808) 935-5021
NANIMAU GARDENS
421 Makalika Street   Tel. (808) 959-3541
RAINBOW FALLS
Wailuku River State Park

Kailua-Kona
ATLANTIS SUBMARINES
Hotel King Kamehameha
75-5660 Palani Road   Tel. (808) 329-6626

Napoopoo
CAPTAIN COOK MEMORIAL

Pahoa
LAVA TREE STATE MONUMENT
Nahawale Forest Reserve

Waimea
KAMUELA MUSEUM
US 19 & US 250   Tel. (808) 885-4724
PARKER RANCH MUSEUM
Parker Ranch Shopping Center   Tel. (808) 885-7655

ISLAND OF KAUAI

Kalaheo
OLU PUA BOTANICAL GARDENS
US 50   Tel. (808) 332-8182

Lawai
PACIFIC TROPICAL BOTANICAL GARDENS
Hailima Road   Tel. (808) 332-7361

Lihue
KAUAI MUSEUM
4428 Rice Street   Tel. (808) 245-6931
SOUTH SEA HELICOPTER TOURS
Tel. (808) 245-7781

Wailua
SMITH'S TROPICAL PARADISE
174 Wailua Road   Tel. (808) 822-5213

ISLAND OF MAUI

HALEAKALA NATIONAL PARK
Tel. (808) 572-9306

Hana
HANA CULTURAL CENTER
US 360   Tel. (808) 248-8622

Kaanapali
WHALER'S VILLAGE & MUSEUM
US 30

Lahaina
CARTHAGINIAN II FLOATING MUSEUM
Tel. (808) 661-8527
LAHAINA ART GALLERY
Front Street   Tel. (808) 667-2152
LAHAINA-KAANAPALI & PACIFIC RAILROAD
US 3C   Tel. (808) 661-0080
WHALER'S VILLAGE
505 Front Street

Waikapu
MAUI PLANTATION   (Tours)
US 30   Tel. (808) 244-7643

Wailuku
MAUI HISTORICAL SOCIETY MUSEUM
2375-A Main Street   Tel. (808) 244-3326

ISLAND OF OAHU

Honolulu
ALOHA TOWER & MARITIME MUSEUM
Ala Moana Boulevard & Bishop Street (pier 8)
Tel. (808) 536-6373
BISHOP MUSEUM
1525 Bernice Street   Tel. (808) 847-3511
FOSTER BOTANIC GARDEN
180 North Vineyard Boulevard   Tel. (808) 533-3214
HONOLULU ACADEMY OF ARTS
900 South Beretania Street   Tel. (808) 538-1006

HONOLULU ZOO
151 Kapahulu Avenue   Tel. (808) 971-7171
JOLANI PALACE STATE MONUMENT (1882)
King & Richards Streets   Tel. (808) 522-0832
LYON ARBORETUM
3860 Manao Road   Tel. (808) 988-7378
MISSION HOUSES MUSEUM
553 South King Street   Tel. (808) 531-0481
NATIONAL MEMORIAL CEMETERY OF THE PACIFIC
Puowaina Drive   Tel. (808) 541-1430
Located on the floor of an extinct volcano, contains the graves of
21,000 service personnel killed in World War II.
THE ROYAL GALLERY
Royal Hawaiian Hotel   Tel. (808) 438-8818
STATE CAPITOL
Beretania & Richards Streets
TENNENT ART FOUNDATION
203 Prospect Street   Tel. (808) 531-1987
U.S. ARMY MUSEUM OF HAWAII
Fort DeRussy   Tel. (808) 438-2821
WAIKIKI AQUARIUM
2777 Kalakaua Avenue   Tel. (808) 923-9741

Laie
POLYNESIAN CULTURAL CENTER
US 83   Tel. (808) 293-3333

Mokuleia
GLIDER RIDES
Tel. (808) 677-3404

Pearl Harbor
SUBMARINE MEMORIAL PARK
Tel. (808) 423-1341

U.S.S. ARIZONA MEMORIAL
US 99   Tel. (808) 422-0561
This memorial is dedicated to the more than 1,170 servicemen who are entombed in the sunken hull of this battleship during the surprise attack by the Japanese on December 7, 1941.

Waimanalo Beach
SEA LIFE PARK
Makapuu Point on US 72   Tel. (808) 259-7933

IDAHO

Jewish people came to Idaho as early as 1861, before the territory was even established, as miners, among Federal troops protecting prospectors and wagon trains, and as merchants hoping to find business that would prosper in this new territory. Mining of gold and silver was in full swing and Jews came, as did many other immigrants, to begin a new life.

Pioneer Jewish families, their descendants still residents of Idaho today, quickly established themselves in their communities. Moses Alexander and David and Nathan Falk are well known because of their mercantile stores, still in business today.

Moses Alexander became a prominent leader in Boise and throughout the state. He served two terms as Boise's mayor and two as Idaho's governor - the first elected Jewish governor in the United States!

Until 1895, Jews in Idaho's scattered communities worshipped in private homes, Odd Fellows halls or other public buildings. In 1895, Moses Alexander and the Jewish men and women in Boise of Western European extraction, decided to establish a synagogue. Congregation Beth Israel was incorporated that year. The first synagogue was built the following year and was located at the corner of State and 11th Streets. This synagogue is thought to be the oldest one in continuous use west of the Mississippi.

Jewish immigrants entered Idaho steadily from the turn of the century until the 1920s. Families moved to southwest

Idaho communities of Twin Falls, Nampa, Caldwell, Weiser, Mountain Home, Idaho City, Silver City, Hailey and Ketchum, as well as Boise.

In 1913, a second synagogue was established in Idaho. Congregation Ahavath Israel was organized primarily by Conservative and Orthodox Jews who came from Eastern Europe. The synagogue was built in 1949 at 1610 Bancock Street. The two congregations have merged to become today's Ahavath Beth Israel Congregation.

Boise

ALEXANDER'S RETAIL STORE
820 Main Street

Moses Alexander was a well-established merchant with branch stores in Lewiston and Pocatello. This store is a registered National Historic Landmark.

TEMPLE BETH ISRAEL
1102 State Street   Tel. (208) 342-7247

The oldest synagogue in continuous use west of the Mississippi. It was constructed in 1895. The congregation's first president, Moses Alexander, was a 2-term Boise mayor and served as Idaho's governor from 1915 to 1919, making him the nation's first Jewish governor. The synagogue was modeled after others built in St. Louis during the period and is distinguished by its Romanesque style with Moorish influences. The unusual beauty of its stained-glass windows, the sharp angles of its architectural form and the patterns cast by its rough-hewn, shake shingles all contribute to Temple Beth Israel's historical uniqueness.

FALK'S DEPARTMENT STORE
100 North 8th Street

This is the oldest existing mercantile establishment in Boise. It was started by David, Sigmund and Nathan Falk in 1865. The building is an Historic Landmark.

ALEXANDER HOUSE
304 State Street

Built in 1897 by Moses Alexander, the first Jewish governor of Idaho. The building is listed in the National Historic Registry.

SYNAGOGUES

Boise 83706
Congregation Ahavath Beth Israel   (R)
1102 State Street   Tel. (208) 342-7247
Pocatello   83201
Temple Emanu-El   (R)
306 North 18th Avenue   Tel. (208) 232-4758

First Jewish governor in the United States, Moses Alexander.

OTHER SIGHTS

Arco
EXPERIMENTAL BREEDER REACTOR #1
US 20   Tel. (208) 526-0051
First atomic reactor to generate electricity, built in 1951.

Banks
CASCADE RAFTING COMPANY
Tel. (800) 292-RAFT

Boise
BOISE ART MUSEUM
670 South Julia Davis Drive   Tel. (208) 345-8330
BOISE FIRE CENTER
3905 Vista Avenue   Tel. (208) 389-2458
BOISE TOUR TRAIN
Capitol Boulevard at Julia Davis Park   Tel. (208) 342-4796
IDAHO HISTORICAL MUSEUM
610 North Julia Davis Drive   Tel. (208) 334-2120
OLD IDAHO PENITENTIARY   (1874)
Main Street & Warm Springs Road   Tel. (208) 334-2844
STATE CAPITOL
Jefferson & 6th Streets   Tel. (208) 334-2411
WORLD CENTER FOR THE BIRDS OF PREY
South Cole Road   Tel. (208) 362-3716

Burley
CASSIA COUNTY HISTORICAL MUSEUM
East Main Street   Tel. (208) 678-7172

Coeur d'Alene
MUSEUM OF NORTH IDAHO
15 Northwest Boulevard   Tel. (208) 664-3448

MONTANA

Gold was discovered at Alder Gulch near Virginia City in 1862. By 1864, there were at least 25 Jewish miners and storekeepers in Virginia City. While miners dug out gold, their existence depended on supplies brought in from the east and California by resourceful traders, freighter and merchants, among whom were many Jews. As Alder Gulch's gold thinned out, Virginia City declined and the settlers drifted away to new mining camps.

Louis Herschfield drove wagon trains from Denver and Utah to Virginia City. He sold 26 wagonloads of miners' supplies and sundries for gold dust and set himself up as a banker in Virginia City. Herschfield then expanded into White Sulphur Springs, Fort Benton and Helena. His private bank was the nucleus of the National Bank of Helena.

Montana's first permanent Jewish settlement was made at Helena in 1864, when it was still a roaring mining camp known as Last Chance Gulch. The Hebrew Benevolent Society, founded in Helena in 1866, was Montana's first Jewish organization. Established as a cemetery association, this society also cared for needy Jews and sponsored the Territory's first Jewish worship services beginning in 1867.

Temple Emanu-El, organized in 1887, two years before Montana was admitted to the Union, was Montana's first Jewish congregation. Rabbi Samuel Schulman was Helena's first rabbi. He arrived in 1891 when the congregation dedicated its synagogue. That structure, located at Ewig Street and 10th Avenue, is no longer used as a Jewish house of worship. The few remaining Jews presented the building as a gift to the state. It now houses the State Department of Public Welfare.

There are today small Jewish congregations in Billings, Butte and Great Falls.

Billings

TEMPLE BETH AARON

1148 North Broadway   Tel. (406) 248-6412

The rabbi of this Reform congregation is also the only rabbi available to the Jews of Idaho, large areas of Wyoming, and major portions of the Dakotas. The Beth Aaron Cemetery is located at Broadway and 16th Street.

Butte

CONGREGATION B'NAI ISRAEL

327 West Galena Street   Tel. (406) 782-9330

Butte's Jewish community, once the largest in the state, had its origin in the silver boom of 1875 and in the later copper mining era. Temple B'nai Israel was organized in 1897. Another congregation, Adath Israel, broke ranks from this congregation and became the Orthodox shul. Adath Israel's synagogue building was condemned because the expanding mine tunnels made the structure unsafe. In 1965, the two congregations merged under the name B'nai Israel.

MOUNT MORIAH CEMETERY

Located in the southwest corner of the city, the Mount Moriah Cemetery was established in the 1880s on land donated by a former gold prospector, turned merchant, David Cohen. Adjoining the Jewish section are a Catholic and a Masonic cemetery.

Helena

FIRST SYNAGOGUE IN MONTANA
Temple Emanu-El (Former)
Ewig Street and 10th Avenue

Temple Emanu-El, organized in 1887, two years before Montana was admitted to the Union, was Montana's first Jewish congregation. In 1964, the Jewish community dwindled to just a few families. They presented the old synagogue building as a gift to the state. It now houses the State Department of Public Welfare.

Virginia City

A number of Jewish names can be spotted on the store fronts in this restored gold mining town, vivid reminders of

TEMPLE OF CONGREGATION EMANU-EL, HELENA, MONTANA

Montana Historical Society, Helena.

the days when Jewish prospectors, miners and merchants were among the pioneers of Montana.

SYNAGOGUES

Billings 59101
Congregation Beth Aaron   (R)

1148 North Broadway   Tel. (406) 248-6412

Butte
Congregation B'nai Israel

327 West Galena Street   Tel. (406) 782-9330

Great Falls 59406
Great Falls Hebrew Association - Aitz Chaim   (R)

P.O.Box 6192   Tel. (406) 452-9521

OTHER SIGHTS

Big Sky
YELLOWSTONE RAFT COMPANY
Tel. (406) 995-4613

Billings
OSCAR'S DREAMLAND FARM MUSEUM
Shiloh Road   Tel. (406) 656-0966

WESTERN HERITAGE CENTER
2822 Montana Avenue   Tel. (406) 256-6809
YELLOWSTONE COUNTY HISTORICAL MUSEUM
Logan International Airport   Tel. (406) 256-6811

Bozeman
GALLATIN PIONEERS MUSEUM
301 West Main Street   Tel. (406) 586-5421
MUSEUM OF THE ROCKIES
South 7th Avenue & Kagy Boulevard   Tel. (406) 994-2251

Browning
MUSEUM OF MONTANA WILDLIFE & HALL OF BRONZE
US 2 & US 89   Tel. (406) 338-5425
MUSEUM OF THE PLAINS INDIANS
US 2 & US 89   Tel. (406) 338-2230

Butte
ARTS CHATEAU   (1898)
321 West Broadway   Tel. (406) 723-7600
COPPER KING MANSION
219 West Granite Street   Tel. (406) 782-7580
MINERAL MUSEUM
Park Street   Tel. (406) 496-4414

OLD NUMBER 1 (Streetcar)
Tel. (406) 494-5595
WORLD MUSEUM OF MINING &
HELL-ROARIN' GULCH
Park Street   Tel. (406) 723-7211

Chester
LIBERTY COUNTY MUSEUM
210 2nd Street   Tel. (406) 759-5256

Chinook
BLAINE COUNTY MUSEUM
501 Indiana Street   Tel. (406) 357-2590

Choteau
OLD TRAIL MUSEUM
US 89 & US 287   Tel. (406) 466-5332

Circle
McCONE COUNTY MUSEUM
801 US 200 South   Tel. (406) 485-2414

Columbia Falls   (kids)
BIG SKY WATERSLIDE
US 2 & US 206   Tel. (406) 892-5025

Cooke City
YELLOWSTONE WILDLIFE MUSEUM
US 212   Tel. (406) 838-2265

Hardin
CUSTER BATTLEFIELD NATIONAL MONUMENT
I-90 to exit 510   Tel. (406) 638-2621
Site of massacre of 225 U.S. soldiers in June, 1876.

Deer Lodge
OLD MONTANA PRISON   (1871)
1106 Main Street   Tel. (406) 846-3111
POWELL COUNTY MUSEUM
1193 Main Street   Tel. (406) 846-3294
TOWE FORD MUSEUM
1106 Main Street   Tel. (406) 846-3111
YESTERDAY'S PLAYTHINGS DOLL & TOY MUSEUM
1106 Main Street   Tel. (406) 846-1480

Dillon
BEAVERHEAD COUNTY MUSEUM
15 South Montana Street   Tel. (406) 683-5027

Fort Benton
MUSEUM OF THE UPPER MISSOURI RIVER
Front & 18th Streets   Tel. (406) 622-3766

GLACIER NATIONAL PARK
US 89   Tel. (406) 888-5441

Glasgow
PIONEER MUSEUM
US 2   Tel. (406) 228-8692

Glendive
FRONTIER GATEWAY MUSEUM
Belle Prairie Road   Tel. (406) 365-8168

Great Falls
CASCADE COUNTY HISTORICAL MUSEUM
1400 First Avenue   Tel. (406) 452-3462
C.M. RUSSELL MUSEUM
400 13th Street, North   Tel. (406) 727-8787

MALMSTROM AIR FORCE BASE MUSEUM
2nd Avenue, North   Tel. (406) 731-2705
MEHMKE STEAM MUSEUM
US 87/89   Tel. (406) 452-6571
PARIS GIBSON SQUARE
CENTER FOR CONTEMPORARY ART
14th Street & 1st Avenue, North   Tel. (406) 727-8255

Hamilton
DALY MANSION
251 Eastside Highway   Tel. (406) 363-6004
RAVALLI COUNTY MUSEUM
205 Bedford Street   Tel. (406) 363-3338

Hardin
BIG HORN COUNTY HISTORICAL MUSEUM
Exit 497 on I-90   Tel. (406) 665-1671

Harlowton
UPPER MUSSELSHELL MUSEUM
11 South Central Avenue   Tel. (406) 632-5519

Havre
H. EARL CLACK MUSEUM
US 2   Tel. (406) 265-9913

Helena
FRONTIER TOWN
US 12   Tel. (406) 442-4560
LAST CHANCE GULCH TOUR
Tel. (406) 442-6880
MONTANA HISTORICAL SOCIETY MUSEUM
225 North Roberts Street   Tel. (406) 444-2694
ORIGINAL GOVERNOR'S MANSION   (1884)
304 North Ewing   Tel. (406) 444-2694

Missoula
HISTORICAL MUSEUM AT FORT MISSOULA
Tel. (406) 728-3476
MISSOULA MUSEUM OF THE ARTS
335 North Pattee Street   Tel. (406) 728-0447

Monida
RED ROCKS LAKES NATIONAL WILDLIFE REFUGE
Tel. (406) 276-3347

Polson
POLSON-FLATHEAD HISTORICAL MUSEUM
802 Main Street   Tel. (406) 883-3049
GLACIER RAFT CO.
Tel. (406) 883-5838
MIRACLE OF AMERICA MUSEUM
US 93   Tel. (406) 883-6804

Pompeys Pillar
POMPEYS PILLAR NATIONAL LANDMARK
I-94   Tel. (406) 875-2166

Red Lodge
CARBON COUNTY HISTORICAL MUSEUM
US 212   Tel. (406) 446-3914

Scobey
DANIELS COUNTY MUSEUM
7 County Road   Tel. (406) 487-5965

Shelby
MARIAS MUSEUM OF HISTORY & ART
206 12th Avenue   Tel. (406) 434-2551

Sidney
MON-DAK HERITAGE CENTER
120 3rd Avenue, S.E. Tel. (406) 482-3500

Three Forks
HEADWATERS HERITAGE MUSEUM
Cedar & Main Streets Tel. (406) 285-3495

Townsend
BROADWATER COUNTY MUSEUM
133 North Walnut Street Tel. (406) 266-5252

Virginia City
J. SPENCER WATKINS MEMORIAL MUSEUM
219 West Wallace Street
NEVADA CITY MUSEUM
US 287 Tel. (406) 843-5377

West Glacier
GREAT NORTHERN WHITEWATER FLOAT TRIPS
US 2 Tel. (406) 387-5340

West Yellowstone
MADISON RIVER CANYON EARTHQUAKE AREA
US 287 to Hebgen Lake Tel. (406) 646-7369
MUSEUM OF THE YELLOWSTONE
124 Yellowstone Avenue Tel. (406) 646-7814

Whitehall
LEWIS & CLARK CAVERNS
US 10 Tel. (406) 287-3541

White Sulpher Springs
CASTLE MUSEUM
East Baker Street & 2nd Avenue Tel. (406) 547-3370

NEVADA

Prospectors who found gold in the western slopes of the Sierra Nevada Mountains in 1859 didn't realize that the unfamiliar black substance in the ore was actually silver from the Comstock Lode. Entire towns in California were abandoned as miners, storekeepers, bankers, engineers, and explorers crossed the mountains into what is now Nevada. In 1862 Nevada's first directory listed more than 200 Jews who settled in the new mining towns of Virginia City, Austin, Eureka and Carson City.

Adolph Sutro, a German-born engineer, was one of the pioneers on the Comstock Lode, one of the richest silver and gold ore bodies ever discovered. After studying methods used by the miners, Sutro designed a tunnel into Mount Davidson, from Carson City to the Comstock Lode. This Sutro Tunnel is twelve feet wide, ten feet high and five miles long. It provided ventilation, drainage and an easy method of transporting the mined silver ore.

The first congregation was organized in Virginia City in 1864. There were Hebrew benevolent societies and Jewish cemeteries in Austin, Virginia City and Eureka in 1862. In the 1870s, there were also congregations in Carson City and Reno. After the Comstock silver deposits began giving out, Nevada's population shrank and the Jewish population started moving away.

In 1897, there were only 150 Jews in Nevada. The early congregations went out of existence. There was a brief influx of 300 Jews with the discovery of new silver deposits in Tonopah and Golden in 1903. Reno's Jewish population returned when the city became a major railroad junction. The oldest existing synagogue in the state was built in 1911 in Reno for Temple Emanu-El.

There were only 500 Jews in Nevada until the early 1950s. During the next forty years the population increased to approximately 14,000. The largest Jewish community is presently located in Las Vegas. They are involved in various enterprises relating to the hotels, entertainment and the casinos. There are presently seven congregations in Las Vegas, running the gamut from Reform, Conservative, to Orthodox, Sephardic and even Chabad Lubavitch (chassidic). Las Vegas has a kosher restaurant and a mikveh.

Carson City

BONANZA DAYS HEBREW CEMETERY

This cemetery was founded by Jewish pioneers in the days of the silver boom in the late 1860s.

Dayton

SUTRO TUNNEL

This was the tunnel designed by the German-born Jewish

engineer Adolph Sutro. It was cut five miles into Mount Davidson to the Comstock Lode, one of the richest silver and gold ore bodies ever discovered. It took 13 years to construct and was opened in 1870. Mount Davidson is named after Ben Davidson, a founder of the Virginia City Stock Exchange, and the western agent of the European Rothschilds. Adolph Sutro later moved to San Francisco and became mayor of that city.

Las Vegas

CONGREGATION SHAAREI TEFILA
1331 South Maryland Parkway   Tel. (702) 384-3565

This is the largest Orthodox congregation in Nevada. When the new mikveh was completed in early 1991, the west was experiencing one of the severest droughts. It hasn't rained for five years. The problem was that there was no rainfall which was needed to fill up the mikveh before it could be used. The rabbi and several congregants therefore rode up to the mountains near Lake Tahoe and shoveled several barrels of fresh snow which could be used as an alternative for rain or spring water. They brought it back to the mikveh and dumped the snow into the mikveh trough. When it melted, the water level reached the required (40 se'ah) measurement.

Reno

OLDEST CONGREGATION IN NEVADA
Temple Emanu-El
1031 Manzanita Lane   Tel. (702) 825-5600

The Reno Hebrew Benevolent Society was established in 1879. The society's purpose was to secure a piece of land for a cemetery, assist sick members and, in case of death, provide for a decent internment. That historic cemetery is still extant and has been restored.

The congregation built its first synagogue in 1921 at 426 West Street. It was a two-story brick structure with Gothic windows. It was declared structurally unsafe by the Buildings Department and was demolished in the early 1970s. The lot was sold to the El Dorado Hotel and Casino and is now used as a parking lot.

The present synagogue was built in 1973. The original Gothic stained-glass windows have been removed from the original building and are now incorporated in the present daily chapel and synagogue library. There is an old ceramic tile floor with a large Magen David of questionable origin in front of the synagogue. The plaque says that it originates from an old mikveh floor. However, the details around the Magen David have been used in Mormon designs as well.

The congregation was organized as an Orthodox shul. Following World War II it changed to the Conservative ritual.

KOSHER PROVISIONS

Las Vegas

Jerusalem Kosher Restaurant & Deli
1305 Vegas Valley Drive, #C   Tel. (702) 735-2878

SYNAGOGUES

Lake Tahoe

North Tahoe Hebrew Congregation   (R)
(Meets 2nd Friday monthly at 7:30 p.m.)

South Lake Tahoe   (R)

(Meets 3rd Friday monthly at 7:30 p.m.)

Temple Bat Yam   (R)   *Tel. (916) 577-2803*
(On California side of Lake Tahoe)

Las Vegas   89102

Temple Beth Am   (R)
4765 Brussells Avenue   Tel. (702) 456-7014

Temple Beth Sholom   (C)
1600 East Oakey Boulevard   Tel. 384-5070

Chabad of Southern Nevada   (O)
1805 Ivanhoe Way   Tel. (386-6880 or 387-0303

Temple Emanu-El   (C)
6370 West Flamingo, Suite 15   Tel. 645-2848

Congregation Ner Tamid   (R)
2761 Emerson Avenue   Tel. 733-6292

Congregation Or-Bamidbar   (Sephardic)   (O)
4224 East Desert Inn Road   Tel. 871-8885

.Congregation Shaarei Tefila   (O)
1331 South Maryland Parkway   Tel. 384-3565

Reno   89503

Temple Emanu-El   (C)
1031 Manzanita Lane   Tel. (702) 825-5600

Temple Sinai   (R)   *3405 Gulling Road   Tel. 747-5508*

MIKVEH

Las Vegas
Congregation Shaarei Tefilla
1331 South Maryland Parkway   Tel. (702) 384-3565

Nudelman family house in Wellington, Nevada (ca. 1895).

OTHER SIGHTS

Carson City
BOWERS MANSION PARK
10 miles north on old US 395   Tel. (702) 849-0644
NEVADA STATE RAILROAD MUSEUM
2180 South Carson Street (US 395)   Tel. (702) 687-6953
STATE MUSEUM
Mint Building   Tel. (702) 882-1808

Elko
NORTHEASTERN NEVADA MUSEUM
1515 Idaho Street   Tel. (702) 738-3418
NEVADA NORTHERN RAILWAY MUSEUM
1100 Avenue A   Tel. (702) 289-2085
WHITE PINE PUBLIC MUSEUM
2000 Aultman Street   Tel. (702) 28904710

Fallon
CHURCHILL COUNTY MUSEUM
1050 South Maine Street   Tel. (702) 423-3677

Gabbs
BERLIN-ICHTHYOSAUR STATE PARK
23 miles east via SR 844

Genoa
GENOA COURTHOUSE MUSEUM
Main Street   Tel. (702) 782-4325

GREAT BASIN NATIONAL PARK
BRISTLECONE PINE FOREST
LEHMAN CAVES   Tel. (702) 234-7331

Hawthorne
MINERAL COUNTY MUSEUM
10th & D Streets   Tel. (702) 945-5142

Henderson
CLARK COUNTY HERITAGE MUSEUM
1830 South Boulder Highway   Tel. (702) 455-7955
ETHEL M. CHOCOLATE FACTORY & CACTUS GARDEN
Tel. (702) 458-8864

HOOVER DAM
This dam was built during the Depression years (1931-36) and is designed in the Art Deco style. It is 726 feet tall and blocks off the Colorado River after it passes through the Grand Canyon and created Lake Meade. Elevators carry passengers down to the power-plant for a 35-minute tour.   Tel. (702) 293-8367

Las Vegas
BONNIE SPRINGS RANCH-OLD NEVADA
Blue Diamond Road (Red Rock Canyon)   Tel. (702) 875-4191
Petting zoo, horseback riding and a gunfight.
CIRCUS CIRCUS
A tent-shaped hotel casino on the Strip, featuring continuous live circus acts. Children are permitted on the observation levels only. (Free)
IMPERIAL PALACE AUTO COLLECTION
3535 Las Vegas Boulevard South Tel. (702) 731-3311
Located on the 5th floor of this casino hotel are the collection of more than 200 classic and historic automoblies including Hitler's Mercedes and Howard Hughes' Chrysler.
LAS VEGAS MUSEUM OF NATURAL HISTORY
900 Las Vegas Boulevard North   Tel. (702) 384-3466

THE LIBERACE MUSEUM

1775 East Tropicana   Tel. (702) 798-5595

Yes, a museum devoted to the life of the famed performer, Liberace. On display are lavish costumes, diamond-studded pianos and much more.

THE MIRAGE HOTEL & CASINO

Las Vegas Boulevard South   Tel. (702) 791-7111

The front plaza and lobby areas are designed as lush tropical jungles. There are landscaped waterfalls and even a tropical fish tank in the lobby walls. At dusk, the waterfalls start "erupting" with smoke and fire rising from the waters! This "spectacle" occurs every 15 minutes through the evening.

NEVADA STATE MUSEUM

700 Twin Lakes Drive   Tel. (702) 486-5205

RIPLEY'S BELIEVE IT OR NOT

202 East Fremont Street (Four Queens Hotel)   Tel. (702) 385-4011

WET 'N WILD   (kids)

2600 Las Vegas Boulevard   Tel. (702) 737-3819

Overton

LOST CITY MUSEUM OF ARCHAEOLOGY

Pueblo Grande de Nevada   Tel. (702) 397-2193

VALLEY OF FIRE STATE PARK

14 miles southwest on SR 169

The rough floor and jagged walls contain honeycombed formations of eroded red sandstone that appear to be on fire when reflecting the sun's rays.

Reno

FLEISCHMANN PLANETARIUM

North Virginai Street (University of Nevada)   Tel. (702) 784-4811

HARRAH FOUNDATION NATIONAL
AUTOMOBILE MUSEUM

10 Lake Street   Tel. (702) 333-9300

MINERAL MUSEUM
North Center Street (University of Nevada)   Tel. (702) 784-6987
NEVADA HISTORICAL SOCIETY MUSEUM
1650 North Virginia Street   Tel. (702) 789-0190
WILBUR D. MAY MUSEUM & ARBORETUM
1502 Washington Street   (Ranco San Rafael Park)
Tel. (702) 785-5961

Rhyolite
GHOST TOWN
Located on dirt road 2.5 miles west of Beatty. See the elaborate
railroad depot and a house constructed out of bottles.

Tonopah
CENTRAL NEVADA MUSEUM
Logan Field Road   Tel. (702) 482-9676

Virginia City
THE CASTLE
70 South B Street   Tel. (702) 847-0275
CHOLLAR MINE
South F Street   Tel. (702) 847-0155
Original 1861 Comstock gold and silver mine with square-set
timbering.
MACKAY MANSION
129 D Street   Tel. (702) 847-0173
MARK TWAIN MUSEUM OF MEMORIES
C Street   Tel. (702) 847-0454
NAVADA STATE FIRE MUSEUM
51 South C Street   Tel. (702) 847-0717
PIPER'S OPERA HOUSE
B & Union Streets   Tel. (702) 847-0433
VIRGINIA & TRUCKEE RAILROAD
Tel. (702) 847-0380
Restored rail line from Virginia City to Gold Hill.

NEW MEXICO

The earliest known Jews in what is now New Mexico were Marranos, descendants of the secret Jews who fled to the colonies of Spain and Portugal in the 16th century to escape the Inquisition. A large number of them settled in New Spain which included Mexico, New Mexico, Arizona, southern California and part of western Texas. Several secret Jews in New Spain were tried and burned at the stake in 1601.

The first Jewish settlement in modern New Mexico was in 1846 when Solomon Jacob Spiegelberg established a wholesale and retail merchandise business in Santa Fe. The Seligman brothers, cousins of Spiegelberg, founded the Seligman Brothers Trading Company in 1850. They established branches throughout the New Mexico Territory. Until banks were opened, these Jewish mercantile houses not only sold and distributed goods, but served the Territory's banking needs. When there was a shortage of hard currency, the government permitted the Spiegelbergs to issue scrip which was legal tender throughout the region. The Seligmans were among the founders of the First National Bank.

The first Jewish organization in New Mexico was a B'nai Brith lodge, founded in Albuquerque in 1882. Two years later there were enough Jews in Las Vegas to form Congregation Montefiore, named for Sir Moses Montefiore, whose 100th birthday was being celebrated throughout the world in 1884. In 1886, the congregation erected New Mexico's first synagogue. The second congregation in the Territory was organized in Albuquerque by Albert Grunsfeld in 1886. It was called Temple Albert, in his honor.

The most recent Jewish community was organized in the 1940s in Los Alamos. Jewish scientists working on the first atomic bomb created the Los Alamos Jewish Center following World War II.

Albuquerque

TEMPLE ALBERT
1007 Lead Avenue, S.E.   Tel. (505) 883-1818

This is New Mexico's second oldest congregation. It was organized by Albert Grunsfeld in 1887. The synagogue was built the following year.

Las Vegas

OLDEST CONGREGATION IN NEW MEXICO
Temple Montefiore   (Former)
901 8th Street

The first congregation in the New Mexico Territory was organized in 1884. New Mexico became a state in 1912. The congregation was named in honor of Sir Moses Montefiore.

Spiegelberg brothers were noted merchants and bankers in New Mexico.　　Museum of New Mexico, Santa Fe

Los Alamos

LOS ALAMOS JEWISH CENTER
2400 Canyon Road   Tel. (505) 662-2140

This congregation was founded by Jewish scientists employed at the Atomic Energy Commission's Scientific Laboratory. They were involved in the production of the first atomic bomb during World War II.

Santa Fe

SPIEGELBERG HOUSE
237 East Palace Avenue

This adobe building was built in 1888 for Flora and William Spiegelberg, New Mexico's pioneer Jewish settlers. The building has been declared an official historic landmark.

KOSHER PROVISIONS

Albuquerque
Grocery Emporium
1403 Girard Boulevard, NE   Tel. (505) 265-6771
David Yudin   (Butcher)   *Tel. (505) 268-7376*

SYNAGOGUES

Albuquerque   87110
Congregation Albert   (R)
3800 Louisiana Boulevard N.E.   Tel. (505) 883-1818
Congregation B'nai Israel   (C)
4401 Indian School Road   Tel. 266-0155
Congregation Nahalat Shalom
295 La Plata N.W.   Tel. 344-6773
Las Cruces   88004
Temple Beth El   (R)
Parker Road at Melendres   *Tel. (505) 524-3380*
Los Alamos   87544
Los Alamos Jewish Center   (C)
2400 Cannon Road   Tel. (505) 662-2140
Rio Rancho   87124
Rio Rancho Jewish Center
2009 Grande Boulevard   Tel. (505) 892-8511
Roswell   88201
Congregation B'nai Israel   (C)
712 North Washington Avenue   Tel. (505) 623-2073
Santa Fe   87501
Temple Beth Shalom   (R)
205 East Barcelona Road   Tel. (505) 982-1376
Kehillat Torah Bamidbar
205 East Barcelona Road   Tel. 989-9358

OTHER SIGHTS

Abiquiu
GHOST RANCH LIVING MUSEUM
14 miles N.W. on US 84

Alamogordo
ALAMEDA PARK & ZOO
US 54
SPACE CENTER
2 miles N.E. on US 54   Tel. (505) 437-2840   .

Albuquerque
THE ALBUQUERQUE MUSEUM
2000 Mountain Road   Tel. (505) 243-7255
INDIAN PUEBLO CULTURAL CENTER
2401 12th Street, N.W.   Tel. (505) 843-7270
NATIONAL ATOMIC MUSEUM
Kirkland Air Force Base
Wyoming Boulevard, Building 20358   Tel. (505) 844-8443
NEW MEXICO MUSEUM OF NATURAL HISTORY
Rio Grande Boulevard   Tel. (505) 841-8837
OLD TOWN
2000 Central Avenue, N.W.
RESCUE MUSEUM
Kirkland Air Force Base   Tel. (505) 844-1626

Angel Fire
DAV VIETNAM VETERANS NATIONAL MEMORIAL
US 64

Artesia
HISTORICAL MUSEUM & ART CENTER
505 West Richardson Avenue   Tel. (505) 748-2390

Aztec
AZTEC MUSEUM
125 North Main Street   Tel. (505) 334-9829
AZTEC RUINS NATIONAL MONUMENT
US 550

BANDELIER NATIONAL MONUMENT
US 285, then west on US 502, then south on US 4.
Tel. (505) 672-3861

CAPULIN VOLCANO MONUMENT
30 miles N.E. of Raton   Tel. (505) 278-2201

Carlsbad
CARLSBAD MUSEUM & ART CENTER
Fox Street
CARLSBAD CAVERNS NATIONAL PARK
Tel. (505) 785-2232
There are 21 miles of surveyed subterranean corridors and great chambers. Tours are available.

Chama
CUMBRES & TOLTEC SCENIC RAILROAD
US 17   Tel. (505) 756-2151

Cibola National Forest
SANDIA PEAK AERIAL TRAMWAY
5 miles north of Albuquerque   Tel. (505) 242-9052

Deming
DEMING LUNA MIMBRES MUSEUM
301 South Silver Street   Tel. (505) 546-2382

Espanola
PUYE CLIFF DWELLINGS & COMMUNAL HOUSE RUINS
11 miles west on US 30 and US 5   Tel. (505) 753-7326

Fort Sumner
FORT SUMNER STATE MONUMENT
2 miles east on US 60   Tel. (505) 355-2573

GILA CLIFF DWELLINGS NATIONAL MONUMENT
45 miles north of Silver City   Tel. (505) 536-9461

Grants
NEW MEXICO MUSEUM OF MINING
Santa Fe Avenue   Tel. (505) 287-4802

Hobbs
LEA COUNTY COWBOY HALL OF FAME
New Mexico Junior College - Lovington Highway
Tel. (505) 392-4510

Los Alamos
BRADBURY SCIENCE MUSEUM
Diamond Drive   Tel. (505) 667-4444
FULLER LODGE ART CENTER
2132 Central Avenue   Tel. (505) 662-9331
LOS ALAMOS COUNTY HISTORICAL MUSEUM
Central Avenue   Tel. (505) 662-6272

Mesilla
GADSEN MUSEUM
Boutz/Barker Road   Tel. (505) 526-6293

Raton
RATON MUSEUM
148 South First Street   Tel. (505) 445-8300

Roswell
LT. GEN. DOUGLAS L. McBRIDE MUSEUM
College Avenue & North Main Street   Tel. (505) 622-6755

ROSWELL MUSEUM & ART CENTER
11th & Main Streets   Tel. (505) 624-6744
SPRING RIVER PARK & ZOO
College Boulevard & Atkinson Road   Tel. (505) 624-6760

Santa Fe
FOOTSTEPS ACROSS NEW MEXICO
211 Old Santa Fe Trail   Tel. (505) 982-9297
INSTITUTE OF AMERICAN INDIAN ARTS MUSEUM
1369 Cerrillos Road   Tel. (505) 988-6281
MUSEUM OF FINE ARTS
Lincoln Avenue   Tel. (505) 827-4468
MUSEUM OF INDIAN ARTS & CULTURE
710 Camino Lejo   Tel. (505) 827-8941
MUSEUM OF INTERNATIONAL FOLK ART
706 Camino Lejo   Tel. (505) 827-8350
PALACE OF THE GOVERNORS
Palace Avenue   Tel. (505) 827-6483
NEW WAVE RAFTING COMPANY (Whitewater)
Tel. (505) 984-1444
SANTA FE OPERA
7 miles north on US 84/285   Tel. (505) 982-3851
SOUTHWEST SAFARIS
Tel. (505) 988-4246
WHEELRIGHT MUSEUM OF THE AMERICAN INDIAN
Camino Lejo   Tel. (505) 982-4636

Shiprock
FOUR CORNERS MONUMENT
35 miles N.W.
The only place in the country where four states, Arizona, Utah,
Colorado and New Mexico, meet.

Silver City
MINING MUSEUM
15 miles east on US 152   Tel. (505) 537-3381

OREGON

The founders of Oregon's Jewish community came west with the great rush of immigrants who journeyed over the Oregon Trail and north from California. Mostly immigrants from Germany, these pioneer Jews settled in the Willamette Valley towns of Albany, Salem, Corvalis, Oregon City, Eugene and Portland. The early Jewish settlers played a leading role in the commercial, industrial and civic development in the state.

The first congregation, Beth Israel, was founded in 1858, when Oregon was still a part of the Oregon Territory. The first religious services were held in Portland, in Burke's Hall, which was housed above a livery stable located on First Avenue. Beth Israel has since occupied three facilities. The first synagogue on S.W. 5th and Oak Streets was built in 1859.

By 1887, the congregation had grown sufficiently to justify the building of a larger temple. The property at S.W. 12th and Main Streets was acquired for this purpose. A temple was built in 1889 at a cost of approximately $100,000. The building was a combination of semi-Gothic and Mooresque styles, similar in style to San Francisco's Congregation Emanu-El of 1866. Beth Israel's building was used until it was ravaged by fire on December 29, 1923. That fire was deliberately set by an arsonist.

Beth Israel's present temple, completed in 1928, is considered to be one of the finest examples of Byzantine architecture in the Northwest and is designated a National Historic Landmark. It was designed by Morris H. Whitehouse and Herman Brookman.

Portland's second congregation was Ahavai Sholom. It was founded in 1869. It merged with another early congregation, Neveh Zedek (located at S.W. 6th and Hall Streets) and formed Neveh Sholom in 1960. Neveh Sholom is the oldest Conservative congregation in the Pacific Northwest.

In the 1950s, Portland inaugurated a major Urban Renewal project. The entire downtown area, which included many of the old synagogues and its thriving Jewish community, were forced to vacate. All of those structures, religious and residential, were demolished in order to make way for the new downtown buildings. The Jews scatttered in all directions. Many moved to the area near the Mittleman Jewish Community Center, on Capitol Highway. All that is left of the original neighborhood is the old Meade Street shul, located just south of Freeway 405.

The Jewish population of Oregon is approximately 14,000.

Eugene

FRIENDLY HALL - UNIVERSITY OF OREGON

Sam Friendly settled in Eugene in 1865. He was one of the leaders behind the financing and development of the University of Oregon in 1872, of which he served as trustee until his death in 1915. He was elected mayor of the city from 1893 to 1895. The University's Friendly Hall and Friendly Street are named in his honor.

TEMPLE BETH ISRAEL
42 West 25th Street   Tel. (503) 485-7218

This congregation was established in 1932 in a Victorian house located at 231 West 8th Street. The present temple was constructed in 1952 from an original design by H.H. Waechter. The congregation follows the Conservative ritual.

Jacksonville

FIRST JEWISH CEMETERY IN OREGON

The first Jewish religious services in the state of Oregon are believed to have taken place in 1856 in the gold mining town of Jacksonville, where a group of Jewish merchants gathered at the Odd Fellows Hall to celebrate Rosh Hashanah. As the gold faded in the 1870s, the Jews started moving back to San Francisco. All that remains today are 13 gravestones in the old Jewish cemetery.

BRUNNER BUILDING

J.A Brunner and Brothers was the first Jewish business in Jacksonville. Its solid brick building was not only a mercantile establishment but also served as a shelter during the Rogue River Indian uprising. The Brunner building is still standing and is now used as the Public Library.

Portland

THE OLD NEIGHBORHOOD
Meade Street Shul - Congregation Kesser Israel
135 S.W. Meade Street Tel. (503) 222-1239

Congregation Kesser Israel is the last congregation in the old Jewish section of South Portland. It was originally built as a church around the turn of the century and was purchased by this Orthodox congregation in the 1920s. This is the only Orthodox congregation in Portland. It is located just a few minutes walk from the major hotels in the downtown area.

The only other Orthodox congregation in Portland, the Sephardic Congregation Ahavath Achim, located on S.W. Barbur Boulevard, recently merged with Kesser Israel. That congregation only meets on major Jewish holidays.

Services in the Meade Street shul are held only on Saturday and Sunday mornings. The building has been declared an official historic landmark.

JEWISH SHELTER HOME (FORMER)
4133 S.W. Corbett Avenue

This wood-frame building, built around the turn of the century, was owned from 1919 to 1937 by the Jewish Shelter Home. In the course of a year, 18 to 20 children would pass through the house, each staying whatever time was necessary. Oregon Governor Julius Meier, chief executive officer of Meier and Frank Department Store, was the president of the Jewish Shelter Home Board from its beginning through 1933.

The building has been designated an official National Historic Landmark.

NEIGHBORHOOD HOUSE
3030 S.W. Second Avenue

In 1896, the Portland section of the National Council of Jewish Women organized this vocational school. It also contained a religious school. The present brick building was constructed in 1903 and included a sewing school, cooking school, manual training, drawing, basketry and modeling, library, gymnasium and meeting rooms.

In 1906, Portland's largest influx of European immigrants began. To adjust, the Neighborhood House directed itself towards Americanization activities. In more recent years, the National Council of Jewish Women have leased the facilities to local social services groups. The building is listed on the National Register of Historic Places.

TEMPLE BETH ISRAEL
1931 N.W. Flanders Street   Tel. 222-1069

Beth Israel was organized in 1858. Its first building was a "neat frame building, built in the Gothic style with an English-Gothic porch in front." It was built in 1861 and was located at Fifth and Oak Streets. In 1887, the congregation had grown and built its magnificent synagogue designed in semi-Gothic and Mooresque styles. It was located at 12th and Main Streets until fire destroyed it in 1923. Two of the congregation's noted rabbis included Rabbi Stephen S. Wise (1900-1906) and Dr. Jonah B. Wise (1906-1925).

The present temple sits on a 360 by 200 foot lot at 19th and Flanders Streets in northwest Portland. It was built in 1926 in the Byzantine style by architects Morris H. Whitehouse and Herman Brookman.

Beth Israel is the oldest Jewish congregation in the Pacific Northwest. The present temple and its Hebrew school (1230 Main Street) have been listed on the National Register of Historic Places.

Present Congregation Beth Israel, Portland.

Portland's Beth Israel was erected in 1899.

KOSHER PROVISIONS

Portland
Albertson's Supermarket
  5415 S.W. Beaverton-Hillsdale Highway   Tel. (503) 246-1713
Dragoon Deli
Jewish Community Center
  6651 S.W. Capitol Highway   Tel. (503) 244-0111
(Under supervision of local Traditional rabbi)
    (Serves both deli and dairy dishes)
Internatiional Food Bazaar
  915 S.W. 9th   (Downtown)   Tel. 228-1960
Safeway Supermarket
  6745 S.W. Beaverton-Hillsdale Highway   Tel. 292-5111
Strohecker's Market
  2855 S.W. Patton Road   Tel. 223-7391

SYNAGOGUES

Ashland   97520
Temple Emek Shalom   (R)
                    1081 East Main Street   Tel. (503) 488-2909
Havurath Shir Hadash
                              P.O.Box 1262   Tel. 488-7716
Corvalis   97339
Beit Am   - Mid-Willamette Jewish Community Center
                    625 N.W. 36th   Tel. (702) 753-0067
Eugene   97405
Temple Beth Israel   (C)
                    2550 Portland Street   Tel. (503) 485-7218
B'nai B'rith Hillel
              University of Oregon   1414 Kincaid   Tel. 344-7945
Klamath Falls   97603
Klamath Falls Jewish Group
              c/o Annette Comer   6732 Eberlien   Tel. (702) 884-9410
Portland   97201
Congregation Ahavath Achim   (Sephardic)   (O)
                    3225 S.W. Barbur Boulevard   Tel. (503) 227-0010
                    (Meets only on Festivals and High Holy days)
Congregation Beth Israel   (R)
                    1931 N.W. Flanders Street   Tel. 222-1069
Chabad House   (O)
                    14355 S.W. Scholls Ferry Road   Tel. 644-2997
Gesher   *10701 S.W. 25th Avenue   Tel. 452-9238*
Havurah Shalom   (R)
                    6651 S.W. Capitol Highway   Tel. 246-3899
Congregation Kesser Israel   (O)
                    136 S.W. Meade Street   Tel. 222-1239
                    (Meets only on Saturday & Sunday mornings)

Congregation Neveh Shalom   (C)

> *2900 S.W. Peaceful Lane   Tel. 246-8831*

Congregation Shaare Torah   (T)

> *920 N.W. 25th Avenue   Tel. 226-6131*

Roseburg   97429

Umpqua Valley Havurah   *Tel. 459-4700*

Salem   97308

Temple Beth Shalom   (Rec)

> *1795 Broadway N.E.   Tel. (503) 362-5004*

MIKVEH

Portland

Portland Jewish Ritualarium

> *1425 S.W. Harrison Street   Tel. (503) 224-3409*

VOLUME 1.   PORTLAND, OREGON, FRIDAY, AUGUST 10, 1894.   NUMBER 27

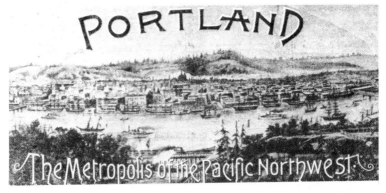

First Jewish newspaper published in Portland.

OTHER SIGHTS

Ashland
WHITEWATER RAFTING
Eagle Sun Tours   Tel. (503) 482-5139

Astoria
CAPTAIN FLAVEL HOUSE
441 8th Street   Tel. (503) 325-2203
COLUMBIA RIVER MARITIME MUSEUM
1792 Marine Drive   Tel. (503) 325-2323
FORT ASTORIA
Exchange & 15th Streets
HERITAGE CENTER MUSEUM
1618 Exchange Street   Tel. (503) 325-2203

Aurora
OLD AURORA COLONY MUSEUM
Liberty & 2nd Streets   Tel. (503) 678-5754

Baker
OREGON TRAIL REGIONAL MUSEUM
Campbell & Grove Streets   Tel. (503) 523-9308
SUMPTER VALLEY RAILROAD
22 miles southwest on SR 7   Tel. (503) 894-2268
U.S.NATIONAL BANK
2000 Main Street   Tel. (503) 523-7791
Exhibit of native gold in all its forms. On display is the 80-ounce
Armstrong Nugget.

Bandon
BANDON HISTORICAL SOCIETY MUSEUM
West First Street   Tel. (503) 347-2164

RIVER'S END GALLERY
First Street (Old Coast Guard Building)
WEST COAST GAME PARK WALK-THRU SAFARI (kids)
7 miles south on US 101.   Tel. (503) 347-3106

Bend
HIGH DESERT MUSEUM
6 miles south on UD 97   Tel. (503) 382-4754
DESCHUTES NATIONAL FOREST
Volcanic region with large craters and lava beds.

Bonneville
BONNEVILLE LOCK & DAM & FISH HATCHERY
I-84 to exit 40   Tel. (503) 374-8393
Brownsville
LINN COUNTY MUSEUM
100 Park Avenue   Tel. (503) 466-3390
MOYER HOUSE
106 Main Street   Tel. (503) 466-3390

Buchanan
OARD'S MUSEUM
US 20 (Main Street)   Tel. (503) 493-2535

Burns
HARNEY COUNTY HISTORICAL MUSEUM
Broadway & D Street

Canyon City
GRANT COUNTY HISTORICAL MUSEUM
Tel. (503) 575-0362
Gold mining town from 1860s.

Estacada
EAGLE CREEK NATIONAL FISH HATCHERY
34288 Southeast Rainbow Road   Tel. (503) 630-6270

Eugene
HULT CENTER FOR THE PERFORMING ARTS
Willamette Street & 6th Avenue   Tel. (503) 687-5000
KERNS ART CENTER
1910 East 15th Avenue
LANE COUNTY HISTORICAL MUSEUM
740 West 13th Avenue   Tel. (503) 687-4239
OREGON RIVER EXPERIENCES
Tel. (503) 689-6198
Rafting excursions.
MUSEUM OF ART
(University of Oregon)   Tel. (503) 686-3027
MUSEUM OF NATURAL HISTORY
(University of Oregon)   Tel. (503) 686-3024
WILLAMETTE SCIENCE & TECHNOLOGY CENTER
2300 Centennial Boulevard   Tel. (503) 687-3619

Florence
DOLLY WARES DOLL MUSEUM   (Kids)
36th Street   Tel. (503) 997-3391
INDIAN FOREST
4 miles north along US 101   Tel. (503) 997-3577
Deer and buffalo roam on the grounds.
SAND DUNES FRONTIER   (kids)
4 miles south on US 101   Tel. (503) 997-3544
Dune-buggy rides and miniature golf.
SEA LIONS CAVES
11 miles north on US 101

Gold Beach
ROGUE RIVER JET BOAT TRIPS
Explore whitewater section of the Rogue River.
Tel. (503) 247-6676 or (800) 451-3645 or (800) 458-3511

Grants Pass
GRANTS PASS MUSEUM OF ART
Riverside Park   Tel. (503) 479-3290

Haines
EASTERN OREGON MUSEUM
4 blocks off US 30

Hells Canyon
HELLS CANYON ADVENTURES
Tel. (800)422-3568
Whitewater rafting outfitters down the Snake River.

Jacksonville
BEEKMAN BANK
California & 3rd Streets
BEEKMAN HOUSE
352 East California Street   Tel. (503) 899-1847
CHILDRENS MUSEUM
Fifth & D Streets   Tel. (503) 899-1847
JACKSONVILLE MUSEUM
Courthouse Building   Tel. (503) 899-1847

JOHN JAY FOSSIL BEDS NATIONAL MONUMENT
8 miles northwest on SR 218   Tel. (503) 575-0721

Klamath Falls
BALDWIN HOTEL MUSEUM
31 Main Street   Tel. (503) 883-4207

FAVELL MUSEUM OF WESTERN ART &
INDIAN ARTIFACTS
125 Main Street   Tel. (503) 882-9996
KLAMATH COUNTY MUSEUM
1451 Main Street   Tel. (503) 883-4208
WEYERHAEUSER LUMBER
US 66   Tel. (503) 884-2241 ext. 353
Tours of lumber manufacturing facility.

Lakeview
HART MOUNTAIN NATIONAL ANTELOPE REFUGE
65 miles northeast
Refuge protects pronghorn antelope, bighorn sheep, mule deer,
bobcat and golden eagle.
SCHMINCK MEMORIAL MUSEUM
128 East E Street

Lincoln City
LACEY'S DOLLHOUSE & MUSEUM
3400 NE US 101   Tel. (503) 994-2392

Monmouth
PAUL JENSEN ARCTIC MUSEUM
590 West Church Street   Tel. (503) 838-8468

MOUNT HOOD
Highest point in Oregon, rising 11,239 feet.

Newberg
HOOVER-MINTHORN HOUSE MUSEUM
South River & East Second Streets   Tel. (503) 538-6629
Home of President Herbert Hoover during his youth.

Newport
HATFIELD-MARINE SCIENCE CENTER
Marine Science Drice   Tel. (503) 867-3011
LINCOLN COUNTY HISTORICAL SOCIETY MUSEUMS
545 S.W. 9th Street
RIPLEY'S-BELIEVE IT OR NOT
250 S.W. Bay Boulevard   Tel. (503) 265-2206
UNDERSEA GARDENS
250 S.W. Bay Boulevard   Tel. (503) 265-2206
YAQUINA ART CENTER
Nye Beach   Tel. (503) 265-5133
YAQUINA BAY LIGHTHOUSE (1871)
Yaquina Bay State Park

OREGON CAVES NATIONAL MONUMENT
20 miles east of Cave Junction on SR 46   Tel. (503) 592-3400
Marble caverns with pillars and stalagtite formations.

Oregon City
JOHN INSKEEP ENVIRONMENTAL LEARNING CENTER
19600 South Molalla   Tel. (503) 657-6958 ext. 351
OREGON TRAIL INTERPRETIVE CENTER
Washington & 5th Streets   Tel. (503) 657-9336
STEVENS-CRAWFORD HOUSE MUSEUM
603 6th Street   Tel. (503) 655-2866

Portland
AMERICAN ADVERTISING MUSEUM
9 N.W. 2nd Avenue   Tel. (503) 226-0000
Portland
CHILDREN'S MUSEUM
3037 S.W. 2nd Avenue   Tel. (503) 248-4587
CRYSTAL SPRINGS RHODODENDRON GARDENS
28th Avenue S.E. near Woodstock   Tel. (503) 796-5193

HOYT ARBORETUM
Washington Park   Tel. (503) 228-8732
JOHN PALMER HOUSE   (1890)
4314 North Mississippi Avenue   Tel. (503) 284-5893
KOIN CENTER
Clay Street & S.W. 3rd Avenue
Portland's television studios (WKOIN) are housed in this skyscraper.
The top floors are the most expensive condominiums in the city.
The city building codes state that no building may be taller than 40
stories since the glorious views of Mount Hood and Mount St.
Helens might be blocked.
LEACH BOTANICAL GARDENS
6704 S.E. 122nd Avenue   Tel. (503) 761-9503
MAVEETY GALLERY
842 S.W. First Avenue   Tel. (503) 224-9442
PORTLAND MUSEUM OF ART
1219 S.W. Park at Jefferson   Tel. 226-2811
OREGON HISTORICAL SOCIETY
1230 S.W. Park Avenue   Tel. (503) 222-1741
OREGON MARITIME CENTER & MUSEUM
113 S.W. Front Street   Tel. (503) 224-7724
OREGON MUSEUM OF SCIENCE & INDUSTRY
4015 S.W. Canyon Road   Tel. (503) 222-2828
THE PORTLAND BUILDING
Main Street & S.W. 4 th Avenue
First major Post-Modern structure in U.S. designed by Michael
Graves in 1982.
PENINSULA ROSE GARDEN
North Ainsworth & North Albina Streets   Tel. (503) 285-1185
PITTOCK MANSION
3229 N.W. Pittock Drive   Tel. (503) 248-4469
WASHINGTON PARK
Burnside Road   Tel. (503) 223-4070
WASHINGTON PARK ZOO
3 miles west on US 26   Tel. (503) 226-1561

TEXAS

After Texas became an independent republic following the Mexican War, its first president, Sam Houston, saw the need for more settlers. He sought a colonization loan from a French bank headed by Henri de Castro, a Jew from Marrano descent. He persuaded Sam Houston that Texas needed people more than money and signed a five-year agreement to colonize a huge area west of San Antonio. Ultimately de Castro brought 2,137 colonists from Alsace-Lorraine between 1844 and 1847 who settled in the towns of Quihi, Vandenberg, D'hanis and Castroville, which was named in his honor.

The first Jewish cemetery in Texas was established in Houston in 1844 and the state's first congregation, Beth Israel, was organized in that city in 1854. While Houston had the first Jewish community in Texas, Galveston, fifty miles southeast on the Gulf of Mexico, had a larger Jewish community until 1880. Galveston was the cultural capital of Texas for much of the 19th century; while people were still shooting each other in gunfights elsewhere in the state, the citizens of Galveston were going to the opera.

In 1866, it was reported that 21 out of 26 merchants in Galveston were Jewish. It remained one of Texas' major cities until it was devastated by a hurricane in 1900. The hurricane that caused the flood killed over 6,000 people! There is now a 17-foot high seawall, running 10 miles along the Gulf Coast. The hurricane and flood drove many Jews out of Galveston. They then settled in Houston and Dallas.

In 1907, Jacob H. Schiff underwrote the Galveston Plan which sought to divert Jewish immigrants from the big eastern cities of New York, Baltimore, Philadelphia and Boston. The immigrants were sent directly from Bremen or Hamburg, Germany to Galveston, where they were met by Rabbi Henry Cohen. Rabbi Cohen was the noted rabbi of Galveston's Congregation B'nai Israel. He arrived in 1888 and served the community for 61 years. The immigrants were fed and housed temporarily in Galveston and then sent on to communities throughout the South and West. This Galveston Plan processed more than 10,000 persons between 1907 and 1914. The project came to an end with the outbreak of World War I.

Houston's Jewish community grew slowly at first, from 17 adults in 1850 to 68 a decade later. These were primarily of German descent. After 1880, Eastern European Jews arrived. The devastating hurricane and flood of 1900 in Galveston brought many Jews into Houston. The Galveston Plan of 1907 brought additional Eastern European immigrants.

Initially, most Jews settled in the First and Second Wards of Houston. They later moved to the Third Ward, near the first site of Congregation Beth Israel, a frame building on LaBranch Street. The East European immigrants at the end of the 19th century tended to move into the Fifth Ward, around Franklin and Navigation, or the Sixth Ward, around Houston and Washington Streets. The Jews have all moved out of these sections.

The second area of settlement, beginning in the 1920s and 1930s, was in Washington Terrace and then Riverside Terrace, along North and South McGregor. This area was home for most of the synagogues and the Jewish Community Center through the end of the 1950s. Some of the former synagogue buildings are still extant but have been sold to local churches or theaters.

The present Jewish community of Houston is located in the southwest section, first to North and South Breaswood Boulevard and later to Meyerland. The Jewish Community Center, the major synagogues and temples and the Hebrew schools are all located in this part of the city. The Jewish population of Houston is approximately 35,000.

In 1872, when Dallas was still a dusty prairie town, 11 merchants organized the Hebrew Benevolent Society which became Congregation Emanu-El two years later. In 1857, Isaac Sanger opened a general store with his four brothers. He later expanded his business and opened stores in Bryan, Calvert, Kosse, Groesbeck and Corsicana. By the mid 1890s Sanger Brothers were doing a million dollar business. The Sangers have long since closed the stores in the small towns and cities, but the Sanger-Harris stores in Dallas stand as a memorial to the mercantile success of five Jewish immigrant brothers.

The world-famous Neiman-Marcus store in Dallas is another success story of an immigrant Jewish family. Herbert Marcus worked for the Sanger Brothers in Dallas as a shoe salesman. He opened his store with his brother-in-law, A.L. Neiman in 1907. The Neiman-Marcus store was the first in the southwest to carry an exclusive line of ladies clothes never before offered in the area and was successful in combining the aspects of a department store with those of a specialty shop. The store is now owned by a merchandising conglomerate with store branches throughout the United States.

The first Jewish community of Dallas settled in the southeast section. All of the original synagogues and temples have been demolished in the 1950s when the city cleared land for its Civic Center and highway expansion. The present Jewish community is located in the northern suburbs near Hillcrest and Northaven Roads. The Jewish population of Dallas is approximately 38,000.

In the years following the Civil War, Jews began to settle in many areas of Texas. Some of these settlements include: Brownsville (1870), Texarkana (1880), El Paso ((1887), San Antonio (1874), Jefferson (1862), Victoria (1885), Waco (1888), Palestine (1886), Beaumont (1894), Austin (1876), Corsicana (1898), Gainesville (1882), Greenville (1890), Marshall (1884) and Calvert (1873). Between 1900 and 1917 many Jewish settlements either dwindled to a handful of residents or vanished entirely. Some of the old synagogue buildings in these towns have been restored and declared historic landmarks.

The oil discoveries before World War I transformed Texas and greatly increased its population, including hundreds of Jewish families from other parts of the country. The World War II military installations that dotted southwest Texas brought an additional Jewish influx that continued into the 1960s and 1970s. The 1980s and early 1990s show a continuous increase in the Jewish population.

Austin

HENRY HIRSCHFELD COTTAGE & HOUSE
303-305 West 9th Street

Henry Hirschfeld was a German-Jewish immigrant, merchant and banker. The buildings were constructed in 1875 and 1885. The house was restored in 1980 and now houses offices. Both have been declared National Historic Landmarks.

Bryan

TEMPLE FREDA (FORMER)
205 Parker Street

This congregation was named for Ethel Freda Kaczer, whose husband, Benjamin, was one of Bryan's leading citizens. The former synagogue was built in 1912 in the Classical Revival style. It has recently been declared a National Historic Landmark.

Calvert

OLD JEWISH CEMETERY

Calvert had a flourishing Jewish community starting in the 1850s. The old Jewish cemetery is located seven blocks from the town center.

Castroville

CASTROVILLE HISTORIC DISTRICT

Henri Castro (1786-1864) was a French-Jewish empressario and founder of the city, which had a population of 700 and 70 houses by 1847, with 34 houses under construction. Castroville now contains 96 historic buildings, mostly built by Alsatian immigrants, of local limestone. The city was founded in 1842. Many of the homes and stores are designed in the Alsatian style.

Corsicana

HISTORIC SYNAGOGUE BUILDING
Temple Beth El (Former)
208 South 15th Street

The earliest Jewish settlers arrived in Corsicana in 1871, the year rail lines were built to the area. In 1898, a group of Reform Jews established Temple Beth El. The wood-frame synagogue was built two years later. The synagogue features two distinctive octagonal towers with onion-shaped domes. Corsicana was the site of a major oil discovery in the early 1890s. The synagogue is now used as a town meeting hall. It has recently been restored and has been declared a Texas Historic Landmark.

Former Temple Beth El, Corsicana.

Dallas

SANGER BROTHERS DRY GOODS STORE (FORMER)
Main and Lamar Streets

Isaac Sanger came to Texas in 1857. His brothers opened dry goods stores throughout the state over the next twenty years. This 8-story steel-frame building with brick veneer, terracotta details is designed as a Commercial and Sullivanesque structure. It was recently sold to the El Centro College and is an official National Historic Landmark.

OLD JEWISH NEIGHBORHOOD

The old Jewish section is now part of the South Boulevard/Park Row Historic District. It dates from around 1913 and contains 116 historic houses built primarily by the city's Jewish community around the old Temple Emanu-El at 1900 South Boulevard. This area is located southeast of Downtown. It has been "cut" by several Freeway ramps. The present Jewish community is located north of the city.

OLDEST SYNAGOGUE IN DALLAS
Temple Emanu-El
Hillcrest & Northwest Highway   Tel. (214) 368-3613

The first congregation in Dallas was organized in 1874. Its first synagogue was dedicated in 1876 and was located near Field and Commerce Streets. Subsequent locations were at Ervay and St. Louis Streets (1899), Harwood and South

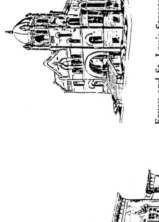

Commerce Street   Dedicated 1877

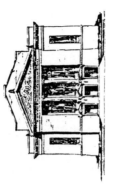

Ervay and St. Louis Streets
Dedicated 1899

Harwood and South Boulevard
Dedicated 1916

Hillcrest and Northwest Highway
Dedicated 1957

Temple Emanu-El of Dallas.

Boulevard (1916), and presently at Hillcrest and Northwest Highway. The present temple was dedicated in 1957. It was designed by Howard R. Meyer and Max M. Sandfield.

The temple complex contains the main chapel, small chapel, Hebrew school, library and social halls. Temple Emanu-El follows the Reform ritual. Family membership is approximately 2375.

HOLOCAUST MEMORIAL
7900 Northaven Road   Tel. (214) 750-4654

The Dallas Memorial Center for Holocaust Studies is housed in the lower level of the Jewish Community Center. The entrance to the memorial center is via a stairwell that leads into an old railroad boxcar used to transport Jews to the concentration and death camps during World War II. It was donated by the National Belgian Railway System. There is an exhibition area which contains many original photographs and artifacts relating to the Holocaust. The center also contains a research library. Tours are available by calling in advance.

Hours: Sunday - Friday 10:00 a.m. to 4:00 p.m. (Free)

El Paso

TEMPLE MOUNT SINAI
4408 North Stanton   Tel. (915) 532-5959

In 1964, Sydney Eisenshtat designed a dramatic modern building for Temple Mount Sinai . The synagogue with its soaring arched parabolic white concrete shell seems to spring out of the rocky Texas soil. This theme is repeated in the interior, where the congregation can see the distant mountains through the high glazed arch behind the Ark.

Temple Mount Sinai was organized in 1899. The congregation's former building was located at 906 North El Paso Street and has been designated a National Historic Landmark. That Clasical Revival brick building with fluted Roman Doric columns served as a synagogue until 1927. It was then sold to a Greek church and is now used as a dance studio and cultural center.

Galveston

SECOND OLDEST SYNAGOGUE IN TEXAS
Temple B'nai Israel
3008 Avenue O   Tel. (409) 765-5796

Temple B'nai Israel was organized in 1870. Its first temple building was located at 22nd and Avenue I. The Henry Cohen Community House, erected in 1928 adjoining the temple, was named for Rabbi Henry Cohen who was the congregation's spiritual leader for 62 years (1888-1950). The former synagogue building was sold to a Masonic temple in 1953. That building has been designated an official Texas Historic Landmark. The congregation moved to its present location in that year. Temple B'nai Israel follows the Reform ritual.

Rabbi Dr. Henry Cohen and Temple B'nai Israel, Galveston.

LASKER HOME FOR HOMELESS CHILDREN
1019 16th Street

Built in 1869 in Greek Revival style. It was purchased in 1901 by Morris Lasker, a banker, miller, state senator, philanthropist and orphan. He donated $10,000 in 1911 for the building's renovation. The Lasker Home is a National Historic Landmark.

E.S. LEVY & CO. STORE
2227 Central Plaza

This is one of the few retail establishments in the country owned and operated by the same family for over a century. It was founded in 1877 by Abraham Levy. It has been designated a Texas Historic Landmark.

Note: The name Rosenberg is a common German (non-Jewish) name. There is no Jewish connection to the Rosenberg Library and Rosenberg Street in Galveston.

Houston

OLDEST CONGREGATION IN TEXAS
Congregation Beth Israel
5600 North Breaswood Boulevard   Tel. (713) 771-6221

In 1844, a small group of Jewish pioneers gathered in the small settlement on the banks of Buffalo Bayou and established a Jewish cemetery. Ten years later they organized Congregation Beth Israel, the first Jewish congregation in the

State of Texas.

The first home was in a small room on Austin Street, between Texas and Prairie. It then moved to a frame building one block southwest on LaBranch. In June, 1870, the temple celebrated with a parade down Main Street. More than 1,000 people marched to the music of Schmidt's Brass Band, to lay the cornerstone of the new temple on Franklin Avenue. It was completed four years later.

In 1908, the congregation dedicated another new building. The Romanesque structure at the corner of Lamar and Crawford was called "the handsomest Temple in the States and one of the finest in the South." After World War I, however, the congregation again outgrew its building. In 1925, Beth Israel moved into the temple at the corner of Holman Avenue and Austin Street. That building continues to serve the Houston community as a theater in the Houston Community College Complex. The Classical Revival building has been designated an official National Historic Landmark.

After World War II, urban residents and returning veterans moved to the suburbs, and Houston's Jewish population moved away from the inner city. Beth Israel is now located on North Breaswood, in the heart of Houston's growing Jewish community. The congregation is a member of the Union of American Hebrew Congregations (Reform). There are approximately 1800 family members. The temple complex contains a magnificent sanctuary, religious school, library, exhibition gallery and social halls.

JEWISH COMMUNITY CENTER
5601 South Breaswood Boulevard   Tel. (713) 729-3200

This is the hub of Jewish life in Houston. There are activities for all age groups, children, teenagers, young adults, singles, adults and seniors. The JCC complex also houses the offices of the Jewish Federation of Greater Houston, Bureau of Jewish Education and the Community Relations Committee. The JCC has a kosher restaurant.

MUSEUM OF JUDAICA
Congregation Beth Yeshurun
4525 Beechnut Boulevard   Tel. (713) 666-1881

Beth Yeshurun started in 1887 when a small group of Jews resolved to conduct traditional services according to the Eastern European ritual. There were two "minyanim" which were composed of Galician and Russian immigrants. The two congregation created, Adath Yeshurun and Beth El, ultimately merged in 1946 and became a Conservative Congregation Beth Yeshurun.

Some of the early synagogue buildings were located at Preston and Hamilton, Jackson and Walker (Third Ward), and Southmore Boulevard. This last building was sold to the Houston Independent School District. The present synagogue was built in 1962.

The Museum of Judaica houses Beth Yeshurun's complete collection of religious and historical documents and memorabilia. There is a magnificent sculpture entitled, "The Last March," which was designed as a Holocaust memorial by the noted artist, Nathan Rappaport. This memorial is located in the south lobby and is highlighted by an atrium and waterfall.

The Kaplan Library contains almost 6,000 volumes of Judaica in English, Hebrew and Yiddish.

Jefferson

JEFFERSON PLAYHOUSE
Market and Henderson Streets

Jefferson was once a booming steamboat town. The Jefferson Playhouse was built as a 2-story frame residential structure. It was acquired as St. Mary's Catholic School in 1869. In 1876, the building was purchased by the Sinai Hebrew Congregation. It built an adjoining 2-story frame synagogue. The two buildings were sold in 1954 and now serve as the Jefferson Playhouse.

Madisonville

SHAPIRA HOTEL
209 North Madison Street

This hotel was built in 1904 by Russian Jewish immigrant Sarah Shapira. It was sold to Clara Wills. The building is now the Woodbine Hotel and is a National Historic Landmark.

Nacogdoches

HOYA LIBRARY & MUSEUM
211 South Lanana Street   Tel. (409) 560-5426

This one-story frame house was built by Adolphus Sterne, the noted German Jewish immigrant who was an attorney, city official, financier of the Texas Revolution and Nacogdoches postmaster, in 1830. It was built as a refuge for women and children during Indian raids.

Palestine

OLD JEWISH CEMETERY

All that remains of this once-thriving Jewish community is the old Jewish cemetery. There used to be a Temple Beth Israel, but the building has long since been sold to a local church.

San Antonio

ALAMO-STYLE TEMPLE
Temple Beth El
211 Belknap Place   Tel. (512) 733-9135

In 1855, a Jewish burial ground was purchased. A few years after the Civil War San Antonio was a frontier village with a population largely Mexican. Temple Beth El was established in

1874. The first temple was dedicated in 1875 and was located at Jefferson and Travis. The second temple was erected on the site of the original building in 1903.

The impressive present temple, with its magnificent dome, was built in 1927 by Seutter and Simons. The building displays the local "Spanish" flavor provided by the twisted colonettes and the encrusted decor. The style is reflective of the Alamo, located just one mile from the temple.

Historians have noted that there were as many as eight Jews who fought for Texas independence at the Alamo. Avram Wolf, who came from England in 1835, died with his two sons in the Battle of the Alamo.

Downtown San Antonio, Texas (ca. 1870).

KOSHER PROVISIONS

Dallas

Preizler's Deli

116 Preston Valley Shopping Center   Tel. (214) 458-8896

Reichman's Deli

7517 Campbell Road (The Pavillion Mall)   Tel. 248-3773

Houston

Jerusalem Kosher Center

96-10 Chimney Rock   Tel. (713) 729-5333

Mama's & Papa's Snack Bar

JCC - 5601 South Breaswood   Tel. 721-9311

Three Brothers Bakery

4036 South Breaswood Boulevard   Tel. 666-2551

San Antonio

Nadler's Bakery

1621 Babcock Street   Tel. (512) 340-1021

(Baked goods only are under supervision, not restaurant)

SYNAGOGUES

Abilene   79604
Temple Mizpah   (R)
849 Chestnut Street   Tel. (915) 672-8225

Amarillo   79109
Temple B'nai Israel   (R)
4316 Albert Street   Tel. (806) 352-7191

Austin   78731
Congregation Agudas Achim   (C)
4300 Bull Creek Road   Tel. (512) 459-3287

Temple Beth Israel   (R)
3901 Shoal Creek Boulevard   Tel. 454-6806

Chabad House   (O)   *2101 Nueces Street   Tel. 472-3900*

Bay City
Beth David Center   *3521 7th Street   Tel. (409) 245-7428*

Beaumont   77704
Temple Emanu-El   (R)
1120 Broadway   Tel. (409) 832-6131

Bellaire   77401
Congregation Brith Shalom
610 Bellaire Road   Tel. (713) 667-9201

Brownsville
Temple Beth El   (R)
825 West St. Francis Street   (512) 542-5263

College Station   77842
Congregation Beth Sholom   (R)
P.O.Box 597   Tel. (409) 696-7313

Corpus Christi   78404
Temple Beth El   (R)
4402 Saratoga Avenue   Tel. (512) 857-8181

Congregation B'nai Israel   (C)
3434 Ft. Worth Avenue   Tel. 855-7308

Corsicana   75110
Congregation Agudas Achim   (O)
919 West Park Avenue   Tel. (214) 874-3045
Dallas   75225
Congregation Agudas Achim   *5810 Forest Lane*
Congregation Beth Torah   (C)
720 Lookout Drive   Tel. (214) 234-1542
Chabad House   (O)
7008 Forest Lane   Tel. 361-8600,   991-5031
Temple Emanu-El   (R)
8500 Hillcrest Road   Tel. 368-3613
Congregation Shaare-Tefila   (O)
6131 Churchill Way   Tel. 661-0127
Congregation Shearith Israel   (C)
9401 Douglas Avenue   Tel. 361-6606
Temple Shalom   (R)   *6930 Alpha Road   Tel. 661-1810*   **71**
Congregation Tifereth Israel   (O)
10909 Hillcrest Road   Tel. 691-3611
Denton   76205
Jewish Congregation of Denton   (R)
P.O.Box 1621   Tel. (817) 382-6771
El Paso   79902
Congregation B'nai Zion   (C)
805 Cherry Hill Lane   Tel. (915) 833-2222
Chabad House   (O)
6505 Westwind Drive   Tel. 833-5711
Temple Mt. Sinai   (R)   *4408 North Stanton   Tel. 532-5959*
Fort Worth   76109
Congregation Ahavath Shalom   (T)
4050 South Helen Street   Tel. (817) 731-4721
Congregation Beth El   (R)
207 West Broadway   Tel. 332-7141
Galveston   77550
Congregation Beth Jacob   (C)
2401 Avenue K   Tel. (409) 762-7267

Temple B'nai Israel (R) *3008 Avenue O Tel. 765-5796*

Harlingen 78551

Temple Beth Israel (R)
1702 East Jackson Street Tel. (512) 423-2928

Houston 77096

Congregation Beth Am (C)
1431 Brittmoore Road Tel. (713) 461-7725

Congregation Beth El (R)
2719 Kingsbrook Lane Tel. 980-1310

Congregation Beth Israel (R)
5600 North Braeswood Boulevard Tel. 771-6221

Congregation Beth Rambam (O) (Sephardic)
11333 Breasridge Tel. 723-3030

Congregation Beth Shalom of the Woodlands (R) (77387)
4890 West Panther Creek Tel. 363-4090

Temple Beth Torah of Kingwood (R) (77325)
P.O.Box 5584 Tel. 359-5444

Congregation Beth Yeshurun (C)
4525 Beechnut Boulevard Tel. 666-1881

Congregation Brith Shalom (C)
4610 Bellaire Boulevard Tel. 667-9201

Chabad House & Mikveh (O)
10900 Fondren Road Tel. 777-2000

Chabad House (O)
1955 University Boulevard Tel. 522-2004

Congregation Emanu-El (R)
1500 Sunset Boulevard Tel. 529-5771

Congregation for Reform Judaism (R)
801 Bering Drive Tel. 782-4162

Congregation Shaar Hashalom (C)
16020 El Camino Real Tel. 488-5861

Congregation Shaarei Tsedek (C)
15825 Memorial Drive Tel. 556-6952

Temple Sinai (R)
783 Country Place Drive Tel. 496-5950

United Orthodox Synagogue   (O)
9001 Greenwillow   Tel. 723-3850
Young Israel of Houston   (O)
11521 Bob White Street   Tel. 728-8564
Laredo   78040
Congregation Agudas Achim   (C)
2100 Laredo Street   Tel. (512) 723-4435
Temple Beth El   1720 Bruni Street   Tel. 727-0717
Temple B'nai Israel   (R)
1515 Guerrero Street   Tel. 723-5678
McAllen   78501
Temple Emanu-El   (R)
1803 North Main Street   Tel. (512) 686-9432
Odessa   79761
Temple Beth El   (R)
1501 North Grandview   Tel. (915) 366-3282
Port Arthur   77642
Rodef Shalom Congregation
3948 Procter Street   Tel. (409) 985-7616
San Antonio   78212
Congregation Agudas Achim   (C)
1201 Donaldson Avenue   Tel. (512) 736-4216
Temple Beth El   (R)   211 Belknap Place   Tel. 733-9135
Chabad House   (O)   14535 Bianco Road   Tel. 493-6503
Congregation Rodfei Sholom   (O)
115 East Laurel Street   Tel. 227-3603
Schulenberg   78956
Temple Israel   (R)   508 Baumgarten Street   (512) 798-3669
Sherman   75090
Temple Beth Emeth   (R)
304 North Rusk Street   Tel. (214) 892-9326
Spring   77379
Jewish Community North   (R)
18519 Klein-Church Road   Tel. (713) 376-0016

Texarkana 75501

 Temple Sinai (R)   *1310 Walnut Street   Tel. (214)   792-2394*

Tyler 75702

 Congregation Ahavas Achim   (C)

 3501 South Donybrook Street   Tel. (214) 597-4282

 Temple Beth El   (R)

 1102 South Augusta Avenue   Tel. 597-2917

Victoria 77901

 Temple B'nai Israel   (R)

 606 North Main Street   Tel. (512) 578-5140

Waco 76710

 Congregation Agudath Jacob   (C)

 4925 Hillcrest Drive   Tel. (817) 772-1451

 Temple Rodef Sholom   (R)

 1717 North New Road (41st Street)   Tel. 754-3703

Wharton 77488

 Congregation Shearith Israel (C)

 1821 Old Lane City Road   Tel. (409) 532-1766

Wichita Falls 76308

 Congregation House of Jacob

 3414 Kemp Boulevard   Tel. (817) 692-5476

The Woodlands 77387

 Congregation Beth Shalom   (R)

 P.O.Box 7711   Tel. (713) 363-4090

THE OLD NEIGHBORHOODS - FORMER SYNAGOGUES

Amarillo   Temple B'nai Israel *2224 Taylor Street*
Ardmore   Temple Emeth *Stanley & D Streets*

Austin

Congregation Agudas Achim   *301 East 10th Street*

Temple Beth Israel   *1101 San Jacinto Street*

Baytown   Congregation Knesseth Israel   *100 West Sterling*

Beaumont   Temple Emanu-El   *3150 McFaddin Street*

Breckenridge   Temple Beth Israel   *1317 Cypress Street*

Breham   B'nai Abraham Congregation

Corpus Christi   Temple Beth El   *1315 Craig Street*

Corsicana

Congregation Agudas Achim   *513 West 4th Street*

Temple Beth El   *208 South 15th Street*

Dallas

Temple Emanu-El   *Ervay & St. Louis Streets*

1900 South Boulevard

Congregation Shearith Israel   *528 Jackson Street*

Park Avenue & Eakin Street

Congregation Tifereth Israel   *145 Highland Street*

Denison   Beth Emeth Congregation

El Paso

Congregation B'nai Zion   *1416 North Mesa Avenue*

210 East Cliff Drive

Temple Mt. Sinai   *900 North Oregon Street*

Fort Worth

Congregation Ahavath Shalom   *Hemphill & Jarvis Streets*

1600 West Myrtle Street

Gainesville   United Hebrew Congregation

Galveston

Congregation Ahavas Israel   *29th & Market Streets*

Congregation Beth Jacob   *1107 24th Street*

Temple B'nai Israel   Avenue *I & 22nd Street*

Hempstead   Congregation Heychal Chayim

Houston

Adath Emeth Congregation   *Cleburne & Ennis Streets*

Congregation Adath Yeshurun   *Preston & Hamilton Street*

Congregation Beth Israel   *Cranford & Hamilton Streets*
Holman & Austin Streets
Beth Jacob Congregation   *Cleburne & Hamilton Streets*
Congregation Beth Yeshurun   *3501 Southmore Street*
United Orthodox Synagogue   *4221 South Braeswood Street*
Jefferson
Hebrew Sinai Congregation   *211 West Austin Street*
Kilgore   Beth Sholom Congregation
Lubbock   Temple Shaareth Israel   *2504 69th Street*
1706 23rd Street
McAllen   Temple Emanu-El   *1410 Redwood Street*
Marshall
Temple Moses Montefiore   *209 West Burleson Street*
Mesquite
Beth Israel Congregation   *4805 Gus Thomasson Road*
Palestine   Beth Israel Congregation   *Magnolia Street*
Port Arthur
Rodef Shalom Congregation   *548 Mobile Avenue*
Richardson
Congregation Beth Tsiyon   *401 Canyon Creek Road*
San Anjelo
Beth Israel Congregation   *222 South Chadbourne Street*

San Antonio
Congregation Agudas Achim   *Aubrey & Guilbau Avenue*
Main Avenue & Quincy Street
Temple Beth El   *Travis & Jefferson Streets*
Tyler
Congregation Ahavas Achim   *1014 West Houston Street*
Temple Beth El   *606 West Shaw Street*
Victoria   Temple B'nai Israel   *Forrest Street*
Waco
Congregation Agudath Jacob   *7th & Columbus Streets*
401 North 15th Street
Temple Rodef Sholom   *924 Washington Avenue*

Wharton

Congregation Shearith Israel   *219 Hollis Street*
201 South Rush Street

Wichita Falls

Congregation House of Jacob   *4th & Lamar Streets*
2624 Amherst Street

Temple Israel   *1204 11th Street*

MIKVEHS

Austin
Chabad House Mikveh
2101 Nueces Street   Tel. (512) 478-8222

Dallas
Congregation Tiferet Israel
10909 Hillcrest   Tel. (214) 368-1787

El Paso
Congregation B'nai Zion
805 Cherry Hill Lane   Tel. (915) 833-2222

Fort Worth
Congregation Ahavath Shalom
4050 South Hulen   Tel. (817) 731-4721

Houston
Mikveh Taharas Yisrael
10900 Fondren Road   Tel. (713) 777-2000 or 779-8100
United Orthodox Synagogue
9001 Greenwillow   Tel. 723-3850

San Antonio
Congregation Rodfei Sholom
115 East Laurel Street   Tel. (512) 227-3603

OTHER SIGHTS

Abilene
ABILENE ZOOLOGICAL GARDENS
South 11th Street (Nelson Park)   Tel. (915) 672-9771
BUFFALO GAP HISTORICAL VILLAGE
Route 89   Tel. (915) 572-3365

Albany
FORT GRIFFIN STATE HISTORICAL PARK
15 miles north on US 283

Alpine
MUSEUM OF BIG BEND
Sul Ross State University   Tel. (915) 837-8143

Amarillo
AMARILLO ART CENTER
2200 South Van Buren Street   Tel. (806) 371-5050

Austin
ELISABET NEY MUSEUM
304 East 44th Street   Tel. (512) 458-2255
GOVERNOR'S MANSION
11th & Colorado Streets   Tel. (512) 463-5516
NEIL-COCHRAN MUSEUM HOUSE

2310 San Gabriel Street   Tel. (512) 478-2335
O. HENRY MUSEUM
409 East 5th Street   Tel. (512) 472-1903
TEXAS MEMORIAL MUSEUM
2400 Trinity Street   Tel. (512) 471-1604

Beaumont
ART MUSEUM OF SOUTHEAST TEXAS
500 Main Street   Tel. (409) 832-3432
BABE DIDRIKSON ZAHARIAS MEMORIL MUSEUM
Gulf Street   Tel. (409) 833-4622
EDISON PLAZA MUSEUM
350 Pine Street   Tel. (409) 839-3089
FIRE MUSEUM OF TEXAS
Walnut & Mulberry Streets   Tel. (409) 880-3917
GLADYS CITY-SPINDLETOP BOOMTOWN
Cardinal & University Drives   Tel. (409) 835-0823
JOHN JAY FRENCH HISTORIC HOUSE MUSEUM
2995 French Road   Tel. (409) 898-0348
McFADDIN-WARD HOUSE
1906 McFaddin Avenue   Tel. (409) 832-2134

Big Spring
THE HERITAGE MUSEUM
510 Scurry Street   Tel. (915) 267-8255

Boerne
CASCADE CAVERNS
3 miles south on I-10   Tel. (512) 755-8080Bonham
SAM RAYBURN HOUSE
2 miles west on US 82   Tel. (903) 583-5558

Borger
HUTCHINSON COUNTY MUSEUM
618 North Main Street   Tel. (806) 273-6121

Brackettville
ALAMO VILLAGE MOVIE LOCATION
7 miles north on US 674   Tel. (512) 563-2580

Brownsville
FORT BROWN
600 International Boulevard
STILLMAN HOUSE MUSEUM
1305 East Washington Street   Tel. (512) 542-3929

Burnet
FORT CROGHAM MUSEUM
703 Buchanan Drive   Tel. (512) 756-8281
VANISHING TEXAS RIVER CRUISE
Tel. (512) 756-6986

Canyon
PANHANDLE-PLAINS HISTORICAL MUSEUM
2401 4th Avenue   Tel. (806) 656-2244

Childress
CHILDRESS COUNTY HERITAGE MUSEUM
210 3rd Street, N.W.   Tel. (817) 937-2261

Cleburne
LAYLAND MUSEUM
201 North Caddo   Tel. (817) 641-3321

Clifton
TEXAS SAFARI RANCH
3 miles S.W. of junction US 219 & US 3220   Tel. (817) 675-3658

Corpus Christi
ART MUSEUM OF SOUTH TEXAS
1902 North Shoreline Drive   Tel. (512) 884-3844
CORPUS CHRISTI MUSEUM
1900 North Chaparral   Tel. (512) 883-2852
MUSEUM OF ORIENTAL CULTURE
418 Peoples Street   Tel. (512) 883-2852

Corsicana
PIONEER VILLAGE
900 West Park   Tel. (903) 872-1468

Cresson
PATE MUSEUM OF TRANSPORTATION
3 miles north on US 377   Tel. (817) 332-1161

Crosbyton
CROSBY COUNTY PIONEER MUSEUM
101 Main Street   Tel. (806) 675-2331

Dallas
DALLAS BOTANICAL GARDENS
8617 Garland Road   Tel. (214) 327-8263
DALLAS MUSEUM OF ART
1717 North Harwood   Tel. (214) 922-1200
INTERNATIONAL MUSEUM OF CULTURES
7500 West Camp Wisdom Road   Tel. (214) 709-2406
OLD CITY PARK
1717 Gano Street   Tel. (214) 421-5141
REUNION TOWER-OBSERVATION DECK   (50th floor)
300 Reunion Boulevard   Tel. (214) 651-1234
THE SIXTH FLOOR
411 Elm Street   Tel. (214) 653-6666
Site from which the shots that killed President John F. Kennedy were fired. Located on the sixth floor of the former Texas School Book Depository.
DALLAS MUSEUM OF NATURAL HISTORY
State Fair Park -   US 67/80   Tel. (214) 670-8457
Note: The Dallas Theatre Center is the only theater designed by Frank Lloyd Wright.

El Paso
BORDER PATROL MUSEUM
310 North Mesa Avenue   Tel. 915) 533-1816
EL PASO CENTENNIAL MUSEUM
University of Texas   Tel. (915) 747-5565

EL PASO MUSEUM OF ART
1211 Montana Avenue   Tel. (915) 541-4040
EL PASO MUSEUM OF HISTORY
15 miles S.E. on US 80 and I-10   Tel. (915) 858-1928
EL PASO SCIENCE MUSEUM
303 North Oregon Street   Tel. (915) 542-2990
FORT BLISS REPLICA MUSEUM
Pleasanton Road   Tel. (915) 568-4518
MAGOFFIN HOME STATE HISTORIC SITE (1875)
1120 Magoffin Avenue   Tel. (915) 533-5147
U.S. ARMY AIR DEFENSE ARTILLERY MUSEUM
5000 Pleasanton Road   Tel. (915) 568-5412
WILDERNESS PARK MUSEUM
2000 Trans-Mountain Road   Tel. (915) 755-4332

Fort Stockton
ANNIE RIGGS MEMORIAL MUSEUM
Main & Callaghan Streets   Tel. (915) 336-2167
OVERLAND-BUTTERFIELD STAGE STOP
20 miles east on US 290 and I-10

Fort Worth
AMON CARTER MUSEUM
3501 Camp Bowie Boulevard   Tel. (817) 738-1933
BOTANIC GARDEN
3220 Botanic Garden Drive   Tel. (817) 870-7686
CATTLEMAN'S MUSEUM
1301 West 7th Street   Tel. (817) 332-7064
LOG CABIN VILLAGE
Forest Park   Tel. (817)926-5881

FORT WORTH MUSEUM OF SCIENCE & HISTORY
1501 Montgomery Street   Tel. (817) 732-1631
KIMBELL ART MUSEUM
Will Rogers Road   Tel. (817) 332-8451
MODERN ART MUSEUM OF FORT WORTH
1309 Montgomery Street   Tel. (817) 738-9215
SID RICHARDSON COLLECTION OF WESTERN ART
309 Main Street   Tel. (817) 332-6554
THISTLE HILL (Mansion)
1509 Pennsylvania Avenue   Tel. (817) 336-1212

Fredericksburg
MUSEUM OF THE PACIFIC WAR
340 East Main Street   Tel. (512) 997-4379
PIONEER MUSEUM
309 West Main Street   Tel. (512) 997-2835

Fritch
LAKE MEREDITH AQUATIC & WILDLIFE MUSEUM
104 North Robey   Tel. (806) 857-2458

Galveston
ASHTON VILLA   (1859)
24th & Broadway   Tel. (409) 762-3933
BISHOP'S PALACE   (1893)
1402 Broadway   Tel. (409) 762-2475
CENTER FOR TRANSPORTATION & COMMERCE
123 Rosenberg Street   Tel. (409) 765-5700
THE COLONEL PADDLEWHEELER
22nd Street Wharf   Tel. (409) 763-4666
WILLIAMS HOME   (1839)
3601 Avenue P   Tel. (409) 765-1839
THE ELISSA (Merchant Ship - 1877)
Pier 21, near the Strand   Tel. (409) 763-1877

GRAND OPERA HOUSE (1894)
2020 Post Office   Tel. (409) 765-1894
TREASURE ISLE TOUR TRAIN
Seawall Boulevard at 21st Street   Tel. (409) 765-9564

Harlingen
CONFEDERATE AIR FORCE FLYING MUSEUM
Valley International Airport   Tel. (512) 425-1057
HARLINGEN HOSPITAL MUSEUM
Boxwood & Raintree Streets   Tel. (512) 428-6974
IWO JIMA WAR MEMORIAL
Harlingen Industrial Air Park   Tel. (512) 423-6006
RIO GRANDE VALLEY MUSEUM
Boxwood & Raintree Streets   Tel. (512) 423-3979

Hereford
DEAF SMITH COUNTY HISTORICAL MUSEUM
400 Sampson Street   Tel. (806) 364-4338
NATIONAL COWGIRL HALL OF FAME
515 Avenue B   Tel. (806) 364-5252

Hillsboro
CONFEDERATE RESEARCH CENTER &
AUDIE MURPHY GUN MUSEUM
       Tel. (817) 582-2555

Houston
ANHEUSER-BUSCH BREWERY (Tours)
775 Gellhorn Road   TEl. (713) 670-1695
BAYOU BEND (Mansion)
Westcott Street   Tel. (713) 529-8773
BLAFFER GALLERY
Fine Arts Bldg. - University of Houston   Tel. (713) 749-1329
CONTEMPORARY ARTS MUSEUM
5216 Montrose   Tel. (713) 526-3129

HOUSTON ARBORETUM & NATURE CENTER
4501 Woodway Drive   Tel. (713) 681-8433
HOUSTON FIRE MUSEUM
2403 Milam   Tel. (713) 524-2526
HOUSTON MUSEUM OF NATURAL SCIENCE
1 Hermann Circle Drive   Tel. (713) 526-4273
LYNDON B. JOHNSON SPACE CENTER
Visitor Center   25 miles S.E. on I-45.   Tel. (713) 483-4321
THE MENIL COLLECTION (Art Museum)
1515 Sul Ross   Tel. (713) 525-9400
MUSEUM OF ART OF THE AMERICAN WEST
One Houston Center   (1221 McKinney Street)   Tel. 650-3933
THE MUSEUM OF FINE ARTS, HOUSTON
1001 Bissonet   Tel. (713) 639-7300
MUSEUM OF PRINTING HISTORY
1324 West Clay   Tel. (713) 522-4652
MUSEUM OF TEXAS HISTORY
1100 Bagby Street   Tel. (713) 655-1912
ROTHKO CHAPEL
3900 Yupon Street   Tel. (713) 524-9839
SAN JACINTO BATTLEGROUND
21 miles east on US 225   Tel. (713) 479-2411

Huntsville
SAM HOUSTON MEMORIAL MUSEUM
1836 Sam Houston Avenue   Tel. (409) 295-7824

Irving
NATIONAL MUSEUM OF COMMUNICATIONS
6305 North O'Connor Road   Tel. (214) 556-1234

Jefferson
ANTIQUE DOLL COLLECTION
301 Lafayette Street (Carnegie Library)

ATLANTA (Private Railroad Car)
200 West Austin Street   Tel. (903) 665-2513
BAYOU QUEEN
Jefferson Landing   Tel. (903) 665-2222
EXCELSIOR HOUSE   (1850)
211 West Austin Street   Tel. (903) 665-2513
HOUSE OF THE SEASONS   (1872)
409 South Alley   Tel. (903) 665-3141
JEFFERSON HISTORICAL MUSEUM
223 West Austin Street   Tel. (903) 665-2775

Kerrville
CLASSIC CAR SHOWCASE & WAX MUSEUM
Harper Road   Tel. (512) 895-5655
COWBOY ARTISTS OF AMERICA MUSEUM
Bandera Highway   Tel. (512) 896-2553

Kilgore
EAST TEXAS OIL MUSEUM
Ross Street   Tel. (903) 983-8295
RANGERETTE SHOWCASE MUSEUM
Broadway & Ross Street   Tel. (903) 983-8265

Kingsville
JOHN E. CONNER MUSEUM
Santa Gertrudis & Armstrong Streets   Tel. (512) 595-2819
KING RANCH HEADQUARTERS
US 141   Tel. (512) 592-8055

Lajitas
LAJITAS MUSEUM & DESERT GARDEN
US 170   Tel. (915) 424-3267
OUTBACK EXPEDITIONS
Tel. (915) 371-2490
BIG BEND RIVER TOURS
Tel. (915) 424-3219

Port Isabel
PORT ISABEL LIGHTHOUSE HISTORICAL SITE   (1852)
Maxan & Tarnava Streets

Richmond
FORT BEND MUSEUM
500 Houston Street   Tel. (713) 342-6478

Round Top
HENKEL SQUARE
Restored buildings from the 1840s   Tel. (409) 249-3308
TEXAS STATE RAILROAD HISTORIC PARK
3 miles west on US 84   Tel. (800) 442-8951

San Angelo
FORT CONCHO MUSEUM
213 East Avenue D   Tel. (915) 657-4441

San Antonio
THE ALAMO   (1744)
Tel. (512) 225-1391
SAN ANTONIO ZOOLOGICAL GARDENS & AQUARIUM
Brackenridhe Park   Tel. (512) 734-7183
WITTE MUSEUM
3801 Broadway   Tel. (512) 226-5544
BUCKHORN HALL OF HORNS MUSEUM
Lone Star Brewery - on US 281   Tel. (512) 226-8301
DALE WARREN WILDLIFE EXHIBIT
101 Broadway   Tel. (512) 659-4861
FORT SAM HOUSTON
I-35 and Harry Wurzbach Highway   Tel. (512) 221-4232
HANGER 9-MUSEUM OF FLIGHT MEDICINE
Brooks Air Force Base   Tel. (512) 536-2203
TOWER OF THE AMERICAS-OBSERVATION DECK
Hemisfair Plaza   Tel. (512) 299-8615

HERTZBERG CIRCUS MUSEUM
210 West Market   Tel. (512) 299-7810
IMAX THEATRE
Rivercenter Mall   Tel. (512) 225-4629
LA VILLITA
Villita Street, near South Presa   Tel. (512) 299-8610
MARION KOOGLER McNAY ART MUSEUM
6000 North New Braunfels Avenue   Tel. (512) 824-5368
NATURAL BRIDGE CAVERNS
17 miles N.E. on I-35   Tel. (512) 651-6101
NATURAL BRIDGE WILDLIFE RANCH
Tel. (512) 438-7400
PASEO DEL RIO (RIVERWALK)
SAN ANTONIO BOTANICAL CENTER
555 Funston Place   Tel. (512) 821-5115
SAN ANTONIO MUSEUM OF ART
200 West Jones Avenue (Lone Star Breweryt)   Tel. (512) 226-5544
SPANISH GOVERNOR'S PALACE
Military Plaza, opposite City Hall   Tel. (512) 224-0601
STEVES HOMESTEAD
509 King William Street   Tel. (512) 225-5924

San Marcos
AQUARENA SPRINGS
Tel. (512) 396-8900
WONDER WORLD
I-35 to exit 202   Tel. (512) 392-3760

Saratoga

BIG THICKET MUSEUM
US 770   Tel. (409) 274-5000

Sherman
RED RIVER HISTORICAL MUSEUM
301 South Walnut Street   Tel. (903) 893-7623

Snyder
DIAMOND MUSEUM OF FINE ARTS
907 25th Street   Tel. (915) 573-6311

Sonora
CAVERNS OF SONORA
8 miles N.W. on I-10   Tel. (915) 387-3105

Sulphur Springs
MUSIC BOX EXHIBIT
201 North Davis Street   (City Library)   Tel. (903) 885-4926

Sweetwater
PIONEER CITY COUNTY MUSEUM
610 East 3rd Street   Tel. (915) 235-8547

Temple
RAILROAD & PIONEER MUSEUM
710 Jack Baskin   Tel. (817) 778-6873

Texarkana
TEXARKANA HISTORICAL MUSEUM
Tel. (903) 793-4831

Tyler
GOODMAN MUSEUM
624 North Broadway   Tel. (903) 531-1286
MUNICIPAL ROSE GARDEN
West Front Street   Tel. (903) 593-2131

Uvalde
ETTIE R. GARNER MUSEUM
333 North Park Street   Tel. (512) 278-5018
GRAND OPERA HOUSE
100 West North Street   Tel. (512) 278-4184

KID STUFF

Amarillo
DON HARRINGTON DISCOVERY CENTER
1200 Streit Drive   Tel. (806) 355-9547
STORYLAND ZOO & WONDERLAND PARK
Thompson Park   Tel. (806) 378-4290

Arlington
SIX FLAGS OVER TEXAS
3.5 miles N.E. on US 360   Tel. (817) 265-3356
WET 'N WILD
Lamar Boulevard   Tel. (817) 265-3356

Austin
AUSTIN CHILDREN'S MUSEUM
1501 West 5th Street   Tel. (512) 472-2499
DISCOVERY HALL
401 Congress Avenue   Tel. (512) 474-7616

Brownsville
GLADYS PORTER ZOO
500 Ringgold Street   Tel. (512) 546-2177

Dallas
DALLAS AQUARIUM
State Fair Park   Tel. (214) 670-8441
DALLAS ZOO
Marsalis Park   Tel. (214) 946-5154
SCIENCE PLACE I & II
State Fair Park   Tel. (214) 428-5555
WET 'N WILD
I-635 at Northwest Highway   Tel. (214) 840-0600

El Paso
EL PASO ZOO
4011 East Paisano   Tel. (915) 544-1928

Fort Worth
FORT WORTH ZOO
Forest Park   Tel. (817) 870-7050

Grand Prairie
THE PALACE OF WAX & RIPLEY'S BELIEVE IT OR NOT!
Belt Line Road   Tel. (214) 263-2391

Henderson
DEPOT MESEUM & CHILDREN'S DISCOVERY CENTER
514 High Street   Tel. (903) 657-4303

Houston
ASTROWORLD
9001 Kirby Drive   Tel. (713) 799-1234
CHILDREN'S MUSEUM OF HOUSTON
3201 Allen Parkway   Tel. (713) 522-6873
HOUSTON ZOO & KIPP AQUARIUM
1513 North MacGregor Way   Tel. (713) 525-3300
WATERWORLD
9001 Kirby Drive   Tel. (713) 799-8404

Lubbock
SCIENCE SPECTRUM
5025 50th Street   Tel. (806) 766-7090

New Braunfels
SCHLITTERBAHN (Water Park)
400 North Liberty   Tel. (512) 625-2351

UTAH

In July, 1847 members of the Mormons entered the Salt Lake Valley to claim the Great Basin area as a home and refuge from years of religious persecution. Among the leaders of the Church, Apostle Orson Pratt and member of the Council of the Seventy, Alexander Niebaur, were themselves born Jewish but later converted.

Julius Gerson Brooks and his wife Fanny have, however, been long recognized as the first permanent Jewish residents of Salt Lake City and Utah, coming first in 1854. Other early Jewish settlers include the Watter brothers, the Auerbach brothers and the Topper brothers. Most were employed in commerce or trade, taking advantage of the needs of the growing mining enterprises. They established the first non-Mormon church in Utah, the Young Men's Literary Association and built the Independence Hall. It was built in 1865 at Third South Street, between Main and West Temple. It was used as a part-time Congregational church and as a Jewish house of worship.

In 1867, the Jews and other non-Mormon businessmen sent a petition to Brigham Young decrying his policy of instructing Mormons to shop only at Mormon-owned institutions. The very seriously adverse affect this had upon Gentile businesses prompted many, including Jews, to leave Utah altogether. In Utah, Gentile has come to mean any non-Mormon. Therefore, Jews are considered as Gentiles in Utah!

Brigham Young, the president of the Mormon Church, gave

the Jews a Hebrew burial ground within the city cemetery in 1866. He offered space on Temple Square in the Hall of the Seventies, to Utah's Jews for the 1867 and 1868 High Holidays.

With the coming of the railroad in 1869 some Jews left Salt Lake City for Corrine, where a Gentile center developed. Ogden's Jewish community developed from this group.

The first Jewish congregation in the Intermountain West was organized by B'nai Israel in 1874 in Salt Lake City. It was organized by German Jews. The first synagogue was built in 1883 and was located at Third South and First West. It was a one-story brick structure designed by a local architect/builder, Henry Monheim. That structure is no longer extant.

The congregation erected their second synagogue in 1891 at Fourth East, between Third South and Second South. The Auerbach brothers, leading merchants in Salt Lake City, donated the money for the services of their nephew, the German Kaiser's architect, Philip Meyer. The synagogue was designed as a replica of the Great Synagogue in Berlin. The building was home to the congregation until 1976 when the two remaining Salt Lake City synagogues merged to form Congregation Kol Ami.

When Congregation B'nai Israel voted to accept the Reform ritual in 1895, many members left and organized Congregation Montefiore. It was an Orthodox congregation whose members stemmed from Eastern Europe. It was located at 355 South 300 East and was built in 1903 by the prominent Utah architect Richard Neuhausen. Of particular interest is the fact that the Latter Day Saints Church donated $2,000 to the

Montefiore Congregation toward defraying construction costs.

Salt Lake City's Conservative congregation, Sharey Tzedek, was organized in 1916. Their Second East building (between 8th and 9th South) was designed by a local builder, John E. Anderson. It was dedicated in the presence of Utah's Governor, Simon Bamberger in 1917. The building was sold in 1948.

Ogden's Jewish community was organized in 1890. Simon Bamberger, a Jewish immigrant from Germany, acquired land holdings, mining interests and built the Bamberger Railroad (a private electric inter-urban railroad line). He was elected the first non-Mormon (Gentile) governor of Utah in 1916.

Ogden

CONGREGATION B'RITH SHOLOM
2756 Grant Avenue Tel. (801) 782-3453

Congregation B'rith Sholom's red brick synagogue building was dedicated on August 21, 1921. It has been designated a National Historic Landmark.

Salt Lake City

SIMON BAMBERGER HOUSE
623 East 100 South

This was the residence built by Simon Bamberger, the first

Jewish and non-Mormon (Gentile) governor of Utah. It is a National Historic Landmark.

CONGREGATION KOL AMI

2425 Heritage Way   Tel. (801) 484-1501

This is the only Jewish congregation in Salt Lake City. It was organized in 1873 as Congregation B'nai Israel. It merged with the Montefiore Congregation in 1972 and changed its name to Congregation Kol Ami.

The Jewish Community Center of Salt Lake City is located at 2416 East 1700 South. For information about programs, call (801) 581-0098.

BROOKS ARCADE BUILDING

Named in honor of the first permanent Jewish settler in Utah, Gerson Brooks. The building is listed on the National Register of Historic Landmarks.

CONGREGATION MONTEFIORE (FORMER)

355 South 300 East

This former synagogue was built in 1903 in the Moorish Revival style. It has been designated a National Historic Landmark.

B'NAI ISRAEL CEMETERY

Located in the fashionable Federal Heights (Popperton) section. This was the first Jewish burial ground in Utah. It was established in 1866 on a piece of ground donated by Brigham Young.

Salt Lake City's former Congregation Montefiore.

CONGREGATION SHAREY TZEDEK (FORMER)
833 South 200 East

This building was built in 1916 for the Conservative congregation. It is presently owned by Post 409 of the Veterans of Foreign Wars. The building has been designated a National Historic Landmark.

TEMPLE B'NAI ISRAEL (FORMER)
249 South 400 East

This is the oldest synagogue structure in Utah. It was built in 1891 and was designed to resemble the Great Synagogue in Berlin. The building is listed on the Register of Historic Places.

Former Congregation B'nai Israel, Salt Lake City.

SYNAGOGUES

Ogden 84401
Congregation Brith Sholem
2750 Grant Avenue   Tel. (801) 782-3453
Salt Lake City 84109
Chavurah B'yachad
c/o Joyce Dolcourt   509 East Northmont Way   (84103)
Tel. (801) 364-7060
Congregation Kol Ami   (C/R)
2425 East Heritage Way   Tel. (801) 484-1501

Cohn Brothers Dry Goods Store, Salt Lake City.

OTHER SIGHTS

ARCHES NATIONAL PARK
Tel. (801) 259-8161

Brigham City
BRIGHAM CITY MUSEUM
24 North 300 West Street   Tel. (801) 723-6769

BRYCE CANYON NATIONAL PARK
Tel. (801) 834-5322

CANYONLANDS NATIONAL PARK
Tel. (801) 259-7164

CAPITOL REEF NATIONAL PARK
Tel. (801) 425-3791

Castle Dale
EMERY COUNTY MUSEUM
161 East 100 North Street   Tel. (801) 381-2444

CEDAR BREAKS NATIONAL MONUMENT
Tel. (801) 586-9451

Cedar City
BRAITHWAITE FINE ARTS GALLERY
351 West Center   Tel. (801) 586-5432

DINOSAUR NATIONAL MONUMENT
Tel. (801) 789-2115

Fairfield
CAMP FLOYD & STAGECOACH INN STATE PARK
US 73   Tel. (801) 768-8932

Salt Lake City
BEEHIVE HOUSE
67 East South Temple Street   Tel. (801) 240-2671
FORT DOUGLAS MILITARY MUSEUM (1862)
Wasatch Drive   Tel. (801) 524-4154
HANSEN PLANETARIUM
15 South State Street   Tel. (801) 538-2098
HOGLE ZOOLOGICAL GARDENS
2600 East Sunnyside Avenue   Tel. (801) 582-1631
PIONEER CRAFT HOUSE
3271 South 500 East Street   Tel. (801) 467-6611
PIONEER MEMORIAL MUSEUM
300 North Main Street   Tel. (801) 533-5759Salt Lake City
SALT LAKE ART CENTER
20 South West Temple Street   Tel. (801) 328-4201
OLD CITY HALL
200 North & State Streets   Tel. (801) 533-5681
STATE CAPITOL (1916)
Capitol Hill   Tel. (801) 533-5681
Note: The Mormon Temple is closed to the general public and only
open to people of the Mormon following.
NATURAL HISTORY MUSEUM
University of Utah   Tel. (801) 581-6927
UTAH MUSEUM OF FINE ARTS
University of Utah
UTAH HISTORICAL SOCIETY
Rio Grande   Tel. (801) 533-5755

Springville
SPRINGVILLE MUSEUM OF ART
126 East 400 South Street   Tel. (801) 489-9434

TIMPANOGOS CAVE NATIONAL MONUMENT
US 92   Tel. (801) 756-5238

WASHINGTON

The construction of the Northern Pacific and Great Northern Railroads to Washington in the 1880s and the Alaska Gold Rush of 1898 were major factors in the growth of the Washington Jewish community. Built with the financial backing of the New York based German-Jewish philanthropist Jacob H. Schiff, the railroads opened new towns, stimulated commerce and agriculture, and brought the first sizable numbers of East European Jewish immigrants to the Northwest. The gold discoveries in the Yukon and Alaska made Seattle a boom town where gold prospectors outfitted themselves for the journey north. By 1900, Seattle had become the metropolis and commercial center of the Northwest, and Jews played an important role in its growth.

When Washington was still an undeveloped frontier territory in 1869, President Grant appointed a Jewish Civil War hero, Edward S. Salomon, as the tenth Territorial governor. While Salomon was governor, the only Jewish community of any size was in Spokane where a Jewish cemetery was established in 1872. Jewish religious services were first organized in Seattle in 1887. The oldest existing congregation in the state, Bikur Cholim, was organized in 1889. The following year, Jewish communities were organized in Tacoma, Walla Walla, Everett and Bellingham.

The first Jewish settlement in Spokane dates back to 1879. There were many Jewish traders in the area. Some were called "egg eaters." They were traditional Jews who traded with the

Indians and would not eat meat away from home, so they ate hard boiled eggs, raw fruit and vegetables. The first congregation in Spokane, Temple Emanu-El, was organized in 1892. The first synagogue was located at Third and Madison. When the congregation outgrew that building, it built its second synagogue at Eighth and Walnut in 1920. That neo-classical building is still extant. Temple Emanu-El merged with an Orthodox congregation, Knesset Israel, in 1966 and created Temple Beth Sholom. The congregation follows the Conservative ritual.

In 1902, a group of Sephardic Jews from the islands of Rhodes and Marmara settled in Seattle. There were over 800 in this group by 1913, making it the largest Sephardic community outside of New York. Today, two Sephardic congregations are located in the Seward Park section, Sephardic Bikur Cholim and Congregation Ezra Bessaroth.

The oldest synagogue in the state, Bikur Cholim, is also situated in this part of Seattle. The Ark and bimah from the former synagogue building, located at 17th Street and Yesler Way, have been transferred to the congregation's new wood-frame building on South Morgan Street. There is an eruv only in the Seward Park section, located east of the Boeing Air Field. There are additional Jewish areas near the University of Washington, in Northend and on Mercer Island.

The Jewish population of Seattle is approximately 30,000.

Seattle

OLDEST SYNAGOGUE IN WASHINGTON
Congregation Bikur Cholim-Machzikay Hadath
5145 South Morgan Street Tel. (206) 723-0970

This congregation was founded on Simchas Torah in 1889 as the Chevra Bikur Cholim. It merged with another Orthodox congregation, Machzikay Hadath, in 1971. The old synagogue building on 17th Street and Yeslow was recently sold to the city and is used as a community center. The Ark and bimah from that former synagogue were transferred to the congregation's present location in Seward Park. It is a beautiful mixture of old and new.

The Seattle Mikveh is located on the grounds of the synagogue. There is also an *eruv* located only in this part of Seattle known as Seward Park. The synagogue has a home hospitality committee, which can arrange accommodations and meals for those who wish to visit the community. There are no hotels or motels in the immediate vicinity.

There are two Sephardic congregations located just a few blocks from this synagogue. They were organized around the turn of the century by Sephardic Jews who arrived from the islands of Rhodes and Marmara. Congregation Bikur Cholim-Machzikay Hadath, Congregation Ezra Bessaroth and Sephardic Bikur Cholim Congregation are sister congregations. The rabbis of the three synagogues, jointly, form the Seattle Beth Din, and the Rabbinical Council of Seattle.

FIRST REFORM CONGREGATION
Temple De Hirsch Sinai
1511 East Pike Street Tel. (206) 323-8486

Bikur Cholim is Seattle's oldest congregation.

In 1899, seventy Seattle Jewish families gathered together to raise the sum of $2,400 to organize Seattle's first Reform Jewish congregation. Temple De Hirsch was named for Baron De Hirsch, in honor of the great Jewish philanthropist who did so much to facilitate the colonization of Jews from the persecuted areas of Europe to the new world.

The cornerstone of the new Temple De Hirsch was laid on June 9, 1901, at Boylston and Marion. Only the basement was completed, however, because it soon became evident that the congregation would outgrow the building. The present site at 15th and East Union was begun in 1907, and was completed on May 29, 1908. In 1971, Temple Sinai of Bellevue merged with Temple De Hirsch, forming the current Temple De Hirsch Sinai.

In the 1960s, the congregation built a new temple adjoining the original synagogue site. The Ark from that old building is now housed in the temple's small chapel. There are plans to demolish the old temple building and construct a new day school.

The congregation has a small suburban branch in Bellevue.

THE STROUM JEWISH COMMUNITY CENTER OF GREATER SEATTLE

3801 East Mercer Way, Mercer Island   Tel. (206) 232-7115

This modern facility offers classes such as acting, dance, drawing, fitness, Hebrew, kidnastics, swimming, music, and yoga. There are programs for all age groups, from toddlers to seniors.

Across the street from the JCC is the Conservative

congregation, Herzl-Ner Tamid. Its former three-story brick synagogue was located at 20th Avenue and East Spruce Street. The Herzl Congregation was founded in 1914 and merged with Congregation Ner Tamid in 1970.

There is another JCC located near the University of Washington at 8606 35th Avenue, NE. It is known as the Northend Branch.

Note: Take I-90 from Seattle Center to Mercer Land. You will cross over the Mercer Island Floating Bridge. Since Lake Washington is a glacial lake and is several hundred feet deep, the most inexpensive way of spanning this waterway was by constructing a series of floating concrete spans. Two years ago, the old bridge was being dismantled. During a severe wind storm, the old structure started "sinking!" It was threatening to dislodge and possibly "sink" the adjoining new Mercer Island Floating Bridge. Luckily, the engineers saved the new structure. Parts of the old bridge are still visible from either side of Lake Washington.

Tacoma

TEMPLE BETH EL
5975 South 12th Street   Tel. (206) 564-7101

In 1892, Temple Beth Israel was formed. Its first building was located at South 10th and I Streets. In 1912, the congregation joined the Reform movement and built a beautiful Moorish brick and tile three-story synagogue. That building, built in 1919, is still located at 4th and J Streets. It is now owned by a local church.

In 1909, another congregation, Chevra Talmud Torah was organized and later changed its name to Temple Sinai. Temple Sinai and Beth Israel merged in 1960 and changed its name to Temple Beth El. The modern synagogue was designed by the firm of Robert Billsbrough Price and Partners.

SIDE TRIP

MOUNT ST. HELENS NATIONAL
VOLCANIC MONUMENT
I-5 to Exit 49. Take Route 503 to 90 to 25 to 99 (Windy Ridge)

At 8:32 Sunday morning, May 18, 1980, Mount St. Helens exploded with cataclysmic fury. When an earthquake of magnitude 5 on the Richter Scale shook the mountain, the bulged north side gave way in a giant avalanche of rock, mud, and ice, followed by explosions directed both laterally and vertically. The eruption moved approximately 3/4 of a cubic mile of the mountain, sending the lighter material almost 14 miles straight up into the atmosphere.

A powerful horizontal blast of gas, ash and fragments killed virtually everything in a wide arc extending 10 to 16 miles northeast, north and northwest of the mountain. Trees were either sheared off or uprooted, stripped and charred. Cars and trucks tumbled and broke apart. Plastic melted and metal twisted. The giant avalanche of rock and ice raced down the volcano's north flank, spilling into the valleys of the North and South Forks of the Toutle River. Part of the avalanche smashed into Spirit Lake, covering St. Helens Lodge, youth camps and campgrounds, sloshing water up the ridges and raising the lake bed about 200 feet.

Pyroclastic flows of hot gases, ash and pumice at temperatures up to 1600 degrees Fahrenheit rolled down the mountain at almost 100 miles per hour, searing everything in their path. 34 fatalities had been recorded and 28 people were listed as missing. One couple was killed while watching the mountain from 15 miles away. Many of the victims died from breathing the hot ash-laden air; others were killed by falling trees, mudflows and floods.

The enormous clouds of ash blew east-northeast across Washington, blocking out the sun for hours. The ash that fell in Washington, Idaho and western Montana brought transportation to a virtual halt. Four days after the blast, ash had crossed the country and reached the East Coast. Downtown Yakima street lights came on automatically as the easterly-moving ash curtain eclipsed the bright spring sun. Two inches of ash fell on Portland, Oregon which is only about 90 miles from the volcano.

Geologists have been closely monitoring the volcano. They have noticed that it has started building-up once again! Mount St. Helens could erupt again without warning and blast hot gases, rock fragments, ash or pumice for many miles. Note: Visitors should keep informed on the condition of the volcano while they are near the area.

The best viewing area is at Windy Ridge, which is just five miles from the volcano.

KOSHER PROVISIONS

Bellevue

Brenner Brothers Bakery

12000 Bel-Red Road   Tel. (206) 454-0600

(Baked goods only are under supervision, not restaurant)

Seattle

Kosher Delight

1509 First Avenue   (Downtown)   Tel. (206) 624-4555
                    (Open Monday-Friday 11:00-4:00)

Noah's Grocery

4700 50th Street   (Seward Park)   Tel. 725-4267

Puget Consumers Co-Op

5041 Wilson South   Tel. 723-2720

Varon's Kosher Market

3931 Martin Luther King Way South   Tel. 723-0240

* Safeway Supermarket   (Genessee Street & Rainier Avenue)

* Albertsons Supermarket

* QFC Supermarket

SYNAGOGUES

Aberdeen   98520
Temple Beth Israel   (R)
1254 North L Street   Tel. (206) 532-7485

Bainbridge Island   98110
Bainbridge Island/North Kitsap Chavurah
P.O.Box 11738   Tel. (206) 842-8453

Bellevue
Temple De Hirsch Sinai   (R)
556 124th N.E.   Tel. (206) 454-5085

Bellingham   98225
Congregation Beth Israel   (R)
2200 Broadway   Tel. (206) 733-8890

Bothell   98012
Northshore Jewish Community   (Rec)
18515 92nd Avenue N.E.   Tel. (206) 481-3024

Bremerton   99352
Jewish Community Center   (C)
11th & Veneta Streets   Tel. (206) 373-9884

Everett/Lynwood   98206
Temple Beth Or   (R)
3215 Lombard (P.O.Box 1232)   Tel. (206) 259-7125
Montefiore Congregation
3212 Lumbard Street   Tel. 1-252-8780

Fort Lewis   98433
Jewish Chapel
12th & Liggett Avenue   Tel. (206) 967-6590

Kent
Community Synagogue of South King County
Tel. (206) 248-8894

Mercer Island   98040
Temple B'nai Torah   (R)
6195 92nd Avenue S.E.   Tel. (206) 232-7243

Herzl-Ner Tamid Synagogue   (C)

3700 East Mercer Way   Tel. 232-8555

South Island Jewish Center   (T)   *Tel. 236-2386*

Richland   99352

Congregation Beth Sholom   (C)

312 Thayler Drive   Tel. (509) 943-9457

Olympia   98057

Temple Beth Hatfiloh   (Progressive)

802 South Jefferson   Tel. (206) 754-8519

Port Angeles   98362

Jewish Heritage Group Havurot Na'ot Midbar

662 Black Diamond Road   Tel. 1-452-2471

Port Townsend   98368

Congregation Bet Shira

P.O.Box 891   Tel. 1-385-7744

Seattle   98118

Temple Beth Am   (R)

8015 27th Avenue N.E.   Tel. (206) 525-0915

Congregation Beth Shalom   (C)

6800 35th Avenue N.E.   Tel. 524-0075

Congregation Bikur Cholim-Machzikay Hadath   (O)

5145 South Morgan Street   Tel. 722-4440

Congregation B'nai Torah   (R)

6195 92nd Avenue S.E.   Tel. 232-7243

Capitol Hill Branch Council House

1501 17th Avenue   Tel. 323-0344

Chabad House   (O)   *4541 19th Avenue N.E.   Tel. 527-1411*

Temple De Hirsch Sinai   (R)

1441 16th Avenue   Tel. 323-8486

Congregation Eitz Or   (Egalitarian)   *Tel. 524-1699*

Emanu-El Congregation   (O)

3412 N.E. 65th Street   Tel. 525-1055

Congregation Ezra Bessaroth   (O)

5217 South Brandon Street   Tel. 722-5500

Sephardic Bikur Cholim Congregation   (O)

6500 52nd Avenue South   Tel. 723-3028

Congregation Shaarei Tefilah-Lubavitch   (O)

6803 40th Avenue N.E.   Tel. 525-1323

West Seattle Minyan   (T)

3254 63rd Avenue S.W.   Tel. 935-5461

Spokane 99203

Temple Beth Shalom   (C)

1322 30th Street   Tel. (509) 747-3304

Tacoma 98465

Temple Beth El   (R)

5975 South 12th Street   Tel. (206) 564-7101

Tri-Cities 99352

Congregation Beth Sholom

312 Thayer Drive   Tel. (509) 943-0457

Vancouver 98665

Jewish Community Association of Southwest Washington

1119-D N.E. 95th Street   Tel. (206) 574-5169

Vashon Island 98070

Haverah - Jewish Studies Group

c/o Pamela Schubert Route 2, Box 441   Tel. 1-463-5161

Walla Walla 99362

Congregation Beth Israel   *1815 Hillbrook Drive*

Wenatchee 98801

Wenatchee Jewish Community

609 Sage Hill Drive   Tel. (509) 662-3561

Yakima 98902

Temple Shalom

1517 Brown Avenue   Tel. (509) 453-8988

MIKVEH

Seattle

Congregation Bikur Cholim

5145 South Morgan Street   Tel. (206) 722-9151 or 383-3644

OTHER SIGHTS

Aberdeen-Hoquiam
ABERDEEN MUSEUM OF HISTORY
111 East 3rd Street   Tel. (206) 533-1976
GRAYS HARBOR HISTORICAL SEAPORT
813 Heron Street   Tel. (206) 532-8611
HOOQUIAM'S CASTLE
515 Chenault Avenue   Tel. (206)533-2005
POLSON PARK & MUSEUM
1611 Riverside Avenue   Tel. (206) 533-5862

Anacortes
ANACORTES MUSEUM
1305 8th Street   Tel. (206) 293-1915

Asotin
ASOTIN MUSEUM
3rd & Filmore Streets   Tel. (509) 243-4659

Bellevue
BELLEVUE ART MUSEUM
301 Bellevue Square   Tel. (206) 454-3322

Bellingham
SEHOME HILL ARBORETUM
Western Washington University
WHATCOM MUSEUM OF HISTORY & ART
121 Prospect Street   Tel. (206) 676-6981

Black Diamond
BLACK DIAMOND HISTORICAL MUSEUM
Railroad Avenue & Baker Street   Tel. (206) 886-1168

Carnation
CARNATION FARMS
Tel. (206) 788-1511

Chehalis
CHEHALIS-CENTRALIA RAILROAD
Main Street   Tel. (206) 748-8885
JOHN R. JACKSON HOUSE   (1845)
Tel. (206) 864-2643
LEWIS COUNTY HISTORICAL MUSEUM
599 N.W. Front Street   Tel. (206) 748-0831

Chelan
LAKE CHELAN MUSEUM
Woodin Avenue   Tel. (509) 687-3470

Cashmere
CHELAN COUNTY HISTORICAL MUSEUM
& PIONEER VILLAGE
Tel. (509) 782-3230

Clarkston
SNAKE RIVER BOAT TOURS
Tel. (509) 758-7712

Cle Elum
CLE ELUM HISTORICAL TELEPHONE MUSEUM
221 East First Street   Tel. (509) 674-5958

Coulee Dam
GRAND COULEE DAM
Tel. (509) 633-9265
Most massive concrete structure in the world; it is 550 feet high,
500 wide at its base and 5,223 feet long.

Coupeville
ISLAND COUNTY HISTORICAL MUSEUM
Alexander & Coveland Streets   Tel. (206) 678-6854

Darrington
RIVER RUNNERS NORTHWEST
Tel. (206) 676-4099

Davenport
LINCOLN COUNTY HISTORICAL MUSEUM
Park & 7th Streets   Tel. (509) 725-7021

Eatonville
NORTHWEST TREK (Wildlife Park)
Tel. (206) 832-6116
PIONEER FARM MUSEUM
Ohop Valley Road   Tel. (206) 832-6300

Elbe
MOUNT RAINIER SCENIC RAILROAD
US 7   Tel. (206) 569-2588

Ellensburg
KITTITAS COUNTY HISTORICAL MUSEUM
Pine & East 3rd Streets   Tel. (509) 925-3778

Ephrata
GRANT COUNTY HISTORICAL MUSEUM &
PIONEER VILLAGE
742 North Basin Street   Tel. (509) 754-3334

Everett
BOEING ASSEMBLY PLANT (Tours)
US 526   Tel. (206) 342-4801

SNOHOMISH COUNTY MUSEUM
2915 Hewitt Avenue   Tel. (206) 259-8849

Ferndale
HOVANDER HOMESTEAD   (1903)
Tel. (206) 384-3444
PIONEER PARK
First & Cherry Streets   Tel. (206) 384-3042

Goldendale
KLICKITAT COUNTY HISTORICAL MUSEUM
127 West Broadway   Tel. (509) 773-4303

Grays River
GRAYS RIVER COVERED BRIDGE   (1905)
US 4

Ilwaco
ILWACO HERITAGE MUSEUM
115 S.E. Lake Street   Tel. (206) 642-3446
LEWIS & CLARK INTERPRETIVE CENTER
Fort Canby State Park   Tel. (206) 642-3029

Kelso
COWLITZ COUNTY HISTORICAL MUSEUM
405 Allen Street   Tel. (206) 577-3119
KELSO VOLCANO TOURIST INFORMATION CENTER
105 Minor Road   Tel. (206) 577-8058

Kennewick
WASHINGTON CENTRAL RAILROAD
Canal Drive   Tel. (509) 452-2336

Kirkland
PETER KIRK BUILDING   (1891)
620 Market Street   Tel. (206) 822-7161

Olympia
STATE CAPITOL MUSEUM
211 West 21st Avenue   Tel. (206) 753-2580

OLYMPIC NATIONAL PARK
Tel. (206) 452-4501

Oroville
OLD MOLSON MUSEUM
Molson Road

Othello
OLD HOTEL ART GALLERY
33 East Larch Street   Tel. (509) 488-5936

Pasco
FRANKLIN COUNTY HISTORICAL MUSEUM
305 North 4th Avenue   Tel. (509) 547-3714
SACAJAWEA STATE PARK MUSEUM
US 12 & US 395   Tel. (509) 545-2361

Port Angeles
CLALLAM COUNTY MUSEUM
Lincoln & East 4th Streets   Tel. (206) 452-7831
ITT RAYONER PULP MILL (tours)
Ennis Street   Tel. (206) 457-3391

Port Gamble
OF SEA & SHORE MUSEUM
US 104   Tel. (206) 297-2426
PORT GAMBLE HISTORIC MUSEUM
US 104   Tel. (206) 297-3341

Port Townsend
JEFFERSON COUNTY HISTORICAL MUSEUM
Madison & Water Streets   Tel. (206) 385-1003

ROTHSCHILD HOUSE   (1868)
Franklin & Taylor Streets   Tel. (206) 385-2722

Poulsbo
MARINE SCIENCE CENTER
17771 Fjord Drive N.E.   Tel. (206) 779-5549

Prosser
BENTON COUNTY HISTORICAL MUSEUM
7th & Paterson Avenue   Tel. (509) 786-3842

Puyallup
FRONTIER MUSEUM
2301 23rd Avenue S.E.   Tel. (206) 845-4402
MEEKER MANSION   (1890)
321 Spring Street   Tel. (848-1770

Richland
HANFORD SCIENCE CENTER
825 Jadwin   Tel. (509) 376-6374

Roslyn
ROSLYN MUSEUM
28 Pennsylvania Avenue   Tel. (509) 649-2776

San Juan Islands
OECAS ISLAND HISTORICAL MUSEUM
Eastbound   Tel. (206) 376-4849
WHALE MUSEUM
62 First Street   Tel. (206) 378-4710

Seattle
BURKE MUSEUM
17th Avenue N.E.   (University of Washington)   Tel. (206) 543-5590
CENTER FOR WOODEN BOATS
1010 Valley Street   Tel. (206) 382-2628

COAST GUARD MUSEUM NORTHWEST
Pier 36 on Alaskan Way South   Tel. (206) 286-9608
FRYE MUSEUM
Terry & Cherry Streets   Tel. (206) 622-9250
HENRY ART GALLERY
41st Street, N.E. & 15th Avenue, N.E.   Tel. (206) 543-2280

MUSEUM OF FLIGHT
9404 East Marginal Way South   Tel. (206) 764-5720
MUSEUM OF HISTORY & INDUSTRY
2700 24th Avenue, East   Tel. (206) 324-1126
NORDIC HERITAGE MUSEUM
3014 N.W. 67th Street   Tel. (206) 789-5707
PIER 59
Alaskan Way at foot of Pike Street
PIKE PLACE MARKET
Pike Street & First Avenue   Tel. (206) 682-7453
PIONEER SQUARE HISTORIC DISTRICT
Contains art galleries, antique shops, boutiques, nightclubs, restaurants and sidewalk cafes. Start on First Avenue and work your way down to the Waterfront Streetcar (trolley) on Alaskan Way.
SEATTLE AQUARIUM
Pier 59 at Waterfront Park   Tel. (206) 386-4320
SEATTLE CENTER
Pacific Science Center   Tel. (206) 443-2001
SEATTLE ART MUSEUM
Volunteer Park   Tel. (206) 625-8900
SPACE NEEDLE
Seattle Center   Tel. (206) 443-2100
Centerpiece of 1962 World's Fair rises 520 feet.
SMITH TOWER   (1905) (Observation Deck)
2nd & Yesler Way   Tel. (206) 622-4004
Was once tallest building outside New York City.
WING LUKE ASIAN MUSEUM
407 7th Avenue, South   Tel. (206) 623-5124

WOODLAND PARK ZOO
Phinney Avenue, North   Tel. (206) 789-7919

Sedro Wooley
LAKE WHATCOM RAILWAY
US 9   Tel. (206) 595-2218
PACIFIC NORTHWEST FLOAT TRIPS
Tel. (206) 755-0694
Operates whitewater rafting trips & gold-panning expeditions.

Sequim
OLYMPIC GAME FARM
Ward Road   Tel. (206) 683-4295
SEQUIM-DUNGENESS MUSEUM
US 101   Tel. (206) 683-8110

Snohomish
PIONEER VILLAGE
Pine Avenue & 2nd Street   Tel. (206) 568-2526

Snoqualmie
PUGET SOUND & SNOQUALMIE VALLEY RAILROAD
US 202   Tel. (206) 746-4025

South Bend
PACIFIC COUNTY COURTHOUSE   (1911)
Memorial Drive
PACIFIC COUNTY HISTORICAL MUSEUM
1008 West Robert Bush Drive   Tel. (206) 875-5224

Spokane
CHENEY COWLES MEMORIAL MUSEUM
West 2316 First Avenue   Tel. (509) 456-3931
BING CROSBY LIBRARY
East 502 Boone Avenue

MUSEUM OF NATIVE AMERICAN CULTURE
East 200 Cataldo Street   Tel. (509) 326-4550

Stevenson
SKAMANIA COUNTY HISTORICAL MUSEUM
Vancouver Avenue   Tel. (509) 427-5141

Suquamish
SUQUAMISH MUSEUM
US 305   Tel. (206) 598-3311

Tacoma
FORT LEWIS MILITARY MUSEUM
I-5   Tel. (206) 967-7206
TACOMA ART MUSEUM
12th & Pacific Avenues   Tel. (206) 272-4258
WASHINGTON STATE HISTORICAL SOCIETY MUSEUM
315 North Stadium Way   Tel. (206) 593-2830

Tumwater
HENDERSON HOUSE   (1905)
602 Deschutes Way   Tel. (206) 753-8583

Vancouver
CLARK COUNTY HISTORICAL MUSEUM
1511 Main Street   Tel. (206) 695-4681
COVINGTON HOUSE   (1846)
4201 Main Street   Tel. (206) 695-6750
FORT VANCOUVER NATIONAL HISTORIC SITE
East Evergreen Boulevard   Tel. (206) 696-7655

Vantage
GINKGO PETRIFIED FOREST
Exit 136 on I-90   Tel. (509) 856-2700

Walla Walla
FORT WALLA WALLA MUSEUM COMPLEX

Wenatchee
NORTH CENTRAL WASHINGTON MUSEUM
127 South Mission Street   Tel. (509) 662-5989
ROCKY REACH DAM
US 97   Tel. (509) 663-8121
Watch migrating fish ascend 1700-foot-long fish ladder.
WASHINGTON STATE APPLE VISITOR CENTER
2900 Euclid Avenue

Westport
WESTPORT HISTORICAL MARITIME MUSEUM
2201 Westhaven Drive   Tel. (206) 268-9692

Winthrop
SHAFER MUSEUM
US 20   Tel. (509) 996-2710

Yakima
CENTRAL WASHINGTON AGRICULTURAL MUSEUM
4508 Main Street   Tel. (509) 457-8735
WASHINGTON CENTRAL RAILROAD
1 East Yakima Avenue   Tel. (509) 452-2336
YAKIMA AREA ARBORETUM

Nob Hill Road
YAKIMA TROLLEY RIDE   (1906)
3rd Avenue & Pine Street   Tel. (509) 575-1700
YAKIMA VALLEY MUSEUM
2105 Tieton Drive   Tel. (509) 248-0747

KID STUFF

Birch Bay   (kids)
WILD 'N WET
Birch Bay-Linden Road   Tel. (206) 371-7911

Chelan
SLIDEWATERS
US 97   Tel. (509) 682-5751

Federal Way
ENCHANTED VILLAGE
36201 Enchanted Parkway South   Tel. (206) 838-1700

Kennewick
OASIS WATERWORKS (Amusement Park)
6321 West Canal Drive   Tel. (509) 735-8442

Seattle
FUN FOREST AMUSEMENT PARK
Seattle Center   Tel. (206) 684-7200
SEATTLE CHILDREN'S MUSEUM
Seattle Center   Tel. (206) 441-1767

Spokane
SPLASHDOWN WATERSLIDE PARK
Mission Avenue   Tel. (509) 924-3079
WALK IN THE WILD
Pines Road   Tel. (509) 924-7220

Tacoma
NEVER NEVER LAND
Point Defiance Park   Tel. (206) 591-5845
POINT DEFIANCE ZOO & AQUARIUM
5400 North Pearl Street   Tel. (206) 591-5335

WYOMING

The first Jews to settle in Wyoming was during the construction of the first trans-continental railroad. Before the Union Pacific began laying tracks westward from Nebraska in the 1860s Wyoming was a vast wilderness occupied by Indians, trappers, traders and Federal troops. As Union Pacific Railroad construction crews and surveyors, guarded by troops from constant Indian raids, pressed their track-laying across southern Wyoming, merchants, peddlers, and freighters moved into Cheyenne in anticipation of its becoming a large transportation and commercial center.

Simon Bamberger and Henry Altman became known as two of the builders of Wyoming. They rented tents and shacks, cashed pay vouchers, peddled and drove wagons. Bamberger continued on to Ogden and Salt Lake City, and became the first non-Mormon governor of Utah.

Gold was discovered in the 1870s in the Black Hills. Many more Jewish merchants and shopkeepers supplied the gold mining camp towns. The first Jewish worship services were said to have started in the late 1870s. The first organized congregation, Emanu-El, was organized in Cheyenne in 1888. The first congregation followed the Reform ritual. A second congregation, Mount Sinai, was organized in 1910. It built the first synagogue in the state in 1915. As the Jewish population began to shrink, Emanu-El joined forces with Mount Sinai.

The Homestead Act brought several Jewish farmers into Wyoming around the turn of the century. The Jewish

Agricultural Society assisted these Jewish farmers who settled in such colonies as Chugwater and Huntley. However, most of the Jewish homesteaders left their farms between 1908 and the 1930s and settled in Denver or Cheyenne.

In 1980, there were 310 Jews in Wyoming. This makes Wyoming Jewry the smallest group in the country. The bulk of the Jewish population live in Cheyenne. There are small communities in Casper, Rock Springs, Evanston, Sheridan, Cody, and Laramie.

Cheyenne

IDELMAN MANSION

Built in 1879 by Max Idelman, was cited in newspapers as the most beautiful in Wyoming. An early Jewish pioneer from Poland, Idelman founded the Cheyenne firm of Goodstein, Idelman and Franklin, one of Wyoming's best-known mercantile establishments. The Idelman Mansion was used by President Theodore Roosevelt as a western White House.

OLDEST SYNAGOGUE IN WYOMING
2610 Pioneer Avenue   Tel. (307) 634-3052

Temple Emanu-El, the first congregation in the state, was organized as a Reform congregation in 1888. As the Jewish population in the city began to shrink, Emanu-El joined forces with the city's second congregation, Mount Sinai in 1927. Mount Sinai's present building was erected in 1951. The congregation follows the Traditional ritual.

SYNAGOGUES

Casper 82601
Temple Beth El
        4105 South Poplar   P.O.Box 943   Tel. (307) 237-2330
Cheyenne 82001
Congregation Mount Sinai   (T)
                2610 Pioneer Avenue   Tel. (307) 634-3052
Laramie 82070
Laramie Jewish Community Center   (R)   *P.O.Box 202*

OTHER SIGHTS

Bighorn National Forest
MEDICINE WHEEL
US 14A

Buffalo
JIM GATCHELL MEMORIAL MUSEUM
10 Fort Street

Casper
FORT CASPER MUSEUM
4001 Fort Casper Road   Tel. (307) 235-8462
NICOLAYSEN ART MUSEUM
596 North Poplar Street   Tel. (307) 235-5247
WERNER WILDLIFE MUSEUM
405 East 15th Street   Tel. (307) 235-2108

Cheyenne
CHEYENNE FRONTIER DAYS OLD WEST MUSEUM
North Carey Avenue   Tel. (307) 778-7291
HISTORIC GOVERNOR'S MANSION (1904)
300 East 21st Street   Tel. (307) 777-7878
NATIONAL FIRST DAY COVER MUSEUM
702 Randall Avenue   Tel. (307) 634-5911
For postage stamp enthusiasts.
STATE CAPITOL
Capitol Avenue & 24th Street   Tel. (307) 777-7220
STATE MUSEUM
Central Avenue & 24th Street   Tel. (307) 777-7024

Cody
BUFFALO BILL HISTORICAL CENTER
720 Sheridan Avenue   Tel. (307) 587-4771

CODY NITE RODEO
US 14/16/20   Tel. (307) 587-5155
CODY RAPID TRANSIT (Whitewater rafting)
Tel. (307) 587-3535
OLD TRAIL TOWN
US 14/16/20   Tel. (307) 587-5302

DEVIL'S TOWER NATIONAL MONUMENT
US 24   Tel. (307) 467-5370
A volcanic neck with fluted columns rises 867 feet. Devil's Tower was featured in the Spielberg film, "Close Encounters of a Third Kind."

Douglas
AYRES NATURAL BRIDGE
I-25
WYOMING PIONEERS MUSEUM
State fairgrounds

Dubois
DUBOIS MUSEUM
US 26/287

Encampmemt
GRAND ENCAMPMENT MUSEUM
Tel. (307) 327-5310

Fort Laramie
FORT LARAMIE NATIONAL HISTORIC SITE
Tel. (307) 837-2221

Gillette
COAL MINE TOURS
Amax Coal Co.   Tel. (307) 687-3200
Rawhide Mine   Tel. (307) 682-8081

ROCKPILE MUSEUM
US 14/16   Tel. (307) 682-3388

GRAND TETON NATIONAL PARK
Tel. (307) 733-2220

Green River
SWEETWATER COUNTY HISTORICAL MUSEUM
80 West Flaming Gorge Way   Tel. (307) 875-2611

Greybull
GREYBULL MUSEUM
325 Greybull Avenue

Guernsey
GUERNSEY STATE PARK MUSEUM
Tel. (307) 836-2900

Jackson
FLOAT TRIPS
Tel. (307) 733-6445
JACKSON HOLE AERIAL TRAM
US 390   Tel. (307) 733-2292
JACKSON HOLE MUSEUM
101 North Glenwood Avenue   Tel. (307) 733-2414
OFF THE DEEP END TRAVELS
Tel. (307) 733-8707
Whitewater rafting & bicycle tours.
ROCKY MOUNTAIN MUSHERS
Tel. (307) 733-7388
Sled dog trips.
ROSS BERLIN'S WILDLIFE MUSEUM
862 West Broadway   Tel. (307) 733-4909

WAGONS WEST
Tel. (800) 433-1595
Covered wagon trips.
WAX MUSEUM OF OLD WYOMING
Cache Street   Tel. (307) 733-3112
WILDLIFE OF THE AMERICAN WEST ART MUSEUM
110 North Center   Tel. (307) 733-5771

Lander
FREMONT COUNTY PIONEER MUSEUM
630 Lincoln Street

Laramie
LARAMIE PLAINS MUSEUM
603 Ivinson Avenue   Tel. (307) 742-4448
RICHARD BROTHERS RAFT TRIPS
Tel. (307) 742-7529
ANTHROPOLOGY MUSEUM
University of Wyoming   Tel. (307) 766-5136
GEOLOGICAL MUSEUM
University of Wyoming   Tel. (307) 766-4218

Lusk
STAGECOACH MUSEUM
342 South Main Street

Medicine Bow
COMO BLUFF FOSSIL CABIN
US 30   Tel. (307) 378-2334
MEDICINE BOW MUSEUM
US 30   Tel. (307) 379-2383

Meeteetse
MEETEESE MUSEUM
1033 Park   Tel. (307) 868-2334

Newcastle
ACCIDENTAL OIL CO. (Tour)
Tel. (307) 746-2046
ANNA MILLER MUSEUM
Delaware Street

Pinedale
MUSEUM OF THE MOUNTAIN MAN
Fremont Lake Road   Tel. (307) 367-4101

Powder River
HELL'S HALF ACRE
US 20/26   (Baby Grand Canyon)

Rawlins
CARBON COUNTY MUSEUM
Walnut & 9th Streets   Tel. (307) 324-9611
WYOMING FRONTIER PRISON
Tel. (307) 324-4111

Riverton
RIVERTON MUSEUM
700 East Park Avenue   Tel. (307) 856-2665

Rock Springs
COMMUNITY FINE ARTS CENTER
400 C Street   Tel. (307) 362-6212

Saratoga
GREAT ROCKY MOUNTAIN OUTFITTERS
Tel. (307) 326-8750
SARATOGA HISTORICAL CENTER
Union Pacific Railroad depot (1917)   Tel. (307) 326-5511

Sheridan
BRADFORD BRINTON MUSEUM & HISTORIC RANCH
US 87S to Big Horn turnoff.   Tel. (307) 672-3172

Sundance
CROOK COUNTY MUSEUM
309 Cleveland Street   Tel. (307) 283-3666

Thermopolis
HOT SPRINGS HISTORICAL MUSEUM
700 Broadway   Tel. (307) 864-5183

Wheatland
LARAMIE PEAK MUSEUM
16th Street   Tel. (307) 322-2514

YELLOWSTONE NATIONAL PARK
Tel. (307) 587-9595
Old Faithful Geyser

CANADA

VANCOUVER, British Columbia

The first established Jewish community was in Victoria, composed of English-speaking traders, merchants, and wholesalers who arrived with news of the gold rush in the Cariboo. They gained respect and admiration for their active community participation. An example of this appreciation was the dedication of the first synagogue in 1863, for which the Freemasons laid a cornerstone and the town's political and ethnic group came out to celebrate.

From Victoria, Jews dispersed throughout British Columbia, up the coast of Vancouver Island to the Fraser River gold rush towns, and later to the Klondike gold rush in the Yukon. After 1886, when Vancouver became the terminus of the Canadian Pacific Railroad, it became the center of the Jewish community.

The next group of Jewish settlers arrived from Eastern Europe, coming to Canada to escape religious and economic persecution. They settled in the Strathcona area of Vancouver along with the Italian, Chinese, Japanese and Irish immigrants.

Today, with British Columbia's Jewish population of nearly 26,000, there are several Jewish communities which actively support synagogue life, charitable organizations and cultural affairs. The Vancouver area is home to most of British Columbia's Jews. Today, the majority of Vancouver's Jewish

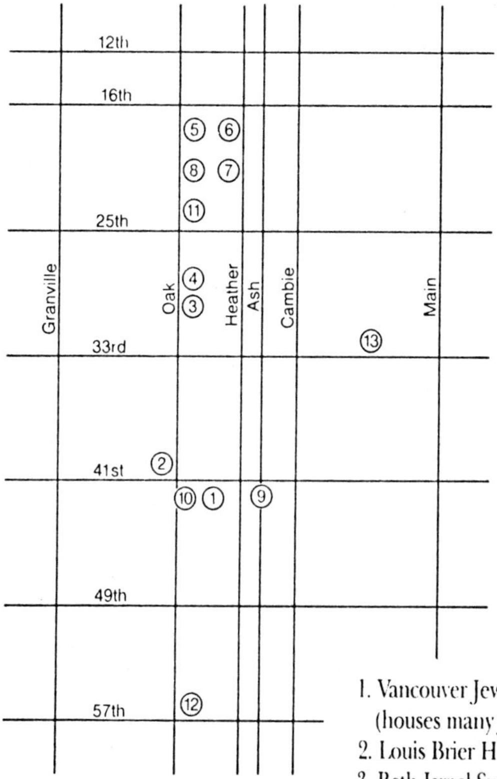
12th
16th
25th
33rd
41st
49th
57th
Granville
Oak
Heather
Ash
Cambie
Main
5
6
8
7
11
4
3
13
2
10
1
9
12

1. Vancouver Jewish Community Centre (houses many Jewish organizations)
2. Louis Brier Home/Hospital
3. Beth Israel Synagogue
4. Talmud Torah
5. Schara Tzedeck Synagogue
6. Beth Hamidrash
7. Jewish Western Bulletin
8. Leon's Kosher Butcher/Bakery
9. Vancouver Peretz Institute
10. Chabad-Lubavitch Centre
11. Shalom Books
12. Temple Sholom
13. Or Shalom Synagogue

VANCOUVER

community resides on the West side of the city, most of its major institutions and facilities are located along Oak Street, south of Broadway.

The Jewish community has a number of active synagogues, Jewish day schools, a Jewish community center, a home for the aged, a community magazine, a weekly Jewish newspaper, and many Jewish social and philanthropic organizations.

Vancouver continues to attract Jewish immigrants from eastern Canada, Israel, South Africa, the Soviet Union and South America. Many young families are settling in the suburbs and developing their own Jewish community services. The communities of Burnaby, Coquitlam, Delta, and Surrey ("Burquest"), also meet their own Jewish needs. The North Shore has a small Jewish population supporting its own synagogue and community center. Richman, perhaps the fastest growing Jewish community, now has two synagogues to serve its people.

Note: There is no eruv in Vancouver.

JEWISH COMMUNITY CENTRE
950 West 41st Avenue   Tel. (604) 266-9111

This is literally the center of Jewish life in Vancouver. There is a full program of classes offered for age groups. The modern building also houses a kosher (vegetarian) snack bar, and offices of the Canadian Jewish Congress, Jewish Immigrant Aid Services, B'nai B'rith, Hadassah, Jewish National Fund, Women's ORT, etc.

THE OLD NEIGHBORHOOD

The old Jewish neighborhood was located in today's Chinatown. Vancouver's first synagogue, Temple Emanu-El, was founded in 1887. In 1907, the Orthodox community organized Sons of Israel. The oldest synagogue building in Vancouver is located at Pender Street and Heatley Avenue (located about one mile east of Main Street and one block south of Hastings Street - Route 7A). That building was recently gutted and rebuilt as a residential condominium. The front façades still display the Judaic symbols. The building has been declared an official historic landmark.

Victoria

OLDEST SYNAGOGUE IN CANADA
Congregation Emanu-El
1461 Blanchard Street   Tel. (604) 382-0615

This is the oldest synagogue in continuous operation since 1863. It has been restored to its original architecture in 1982 and is a Canadian Heritage Site as the oldest standing synagogue in Canada.

Jewish merchants established businesses on lower Yates street in the 1850s. Joseph Boscowitz, the pioneer Jewish fur dealer and entrepreneur, set up his fur store on Wharf and Bastion Streets in 1858. There were also several dry goods and tobacco businesses in the area which were owned by Jews.

The Victoria Hebrew Benevolent Society established the first Jewish cemetery in western Canada. It is still located on Cedar Hill Road.

Victoria's Temple Emanu-El is Canada's oldest congregation.

KOSHER PROVISIONS

Vancouver, British Columbia
Leon's Kosher Meats, Deli & Bakery
3710 Oak Street   Tel. (604) 736-5888
Cafe Mercaz
Jewish Community Centre
950 West 41st Avenue   Tel. (604) 266-9111

SYNAGOGUES

Vancouver, Britsh Columbia
Beth Hamedrash Congregation   (Sephardic) (O)
3231 Heather Street   Tel. (604) 872-4222 or 872-1201
Beth Israel   (C)
4350 Oak Street   Tel. (604) 731-4161
Beth Tikvah Congregation   (C)
9711 Geal Road   Tel. (604) 271-6262
Chabad-Lubavitch   (O)
5750 Oak Street   Tel. (604) 266-1313
Chabad of Surrey Community Center   (O)
 # 210 - 6950 Nicholson Road   Tel. 596-9030
Congregation Eitz Chaim   (O)
8080 Francis Road   Tel. (604) 275-0007
Har El Congregation   (C)
North Shore JCC   1735 Inglewood Avenue   Tel. 922-8245
Louis Brier Home   (O)
1055 West 41st Avenue   Tel. 261-9376
Or Shalom Congregation   (T-Egalitarian)
561 West 28th Avenue   Tel. 872-1614

Congregation Schara Tzedeck   (O)

3476 Oak Street   Tel. 736-7607

Temple Sholom   (R)

7190 Oak Street   Tel. 266-7190

Victoria

Emanu-El Congregation   (C)

1461 Blanchard   Tel. 382-0615

MIKVEHS

Vancouver, British Columbia

Schara Tzedeck Congregation

3476 Oak Street   (V6H 2L8)   Tel. (604) 736-7604

Lubavitch Centre

5750 Oak Street   (V6M 2V7)   Tel. (604) 266-1313

ISRAELI FOLK DANCING

CALIFORNIA

Israeli Folk Dance Grapevine
350 7th Avenue, Box 219   San Francisco , CA 94118
Tel. (415) 668-1487   (Monthly newsletter)
Albany   (Easy Bay)
Veterans Memorial Hall
1325 Portland Avenue
(Darron Feldstein   Tel. (415) 566-0896)
(Harriet Frank   Tel. (415) 524-3258)   Wednesday   8:00 - 12 midnight
Berkeley
Finnish Hall
1819 10th Street   Tel. (415) 525-4974   Sunday   7-10 p.m.
Cotati
Rina Dance Space
6815 Redwood Drive   Tel. (707) 823-0526   Thursday   7 - 9 p.m.
Livermore
Congregation Beth Emek
1886 College Avenue   Tel. (415) 447-8282
Third Saturday of each month   8 - 10 p.m.

Los Angeles & Vicinity
Temple Adat Elohim
2420 East Hillcrest Drive   (Thousand Oaks)
Tel. (805) 497-7101   Tuesday 7:30 - 11:30 p.m.
Adat Shalom
3030 Westwood Boulevard   Tel. (213) 475-4985   Monday   7:30 - 11 p.m.
Temple Akiba
5249 South Sepulveda Boulevard (Culver City)
Tel. (213) 870-6575   Monday   8:15 p.m.
Temple Aliyah
6025 Valley Circle (Woodland Hills)   Tel. (818) 346-3545   Monday   7:30 p.m.

Congregation Beth Chayim Chadashim
6000 West Pico Boulevard   Tel. (213) 931-7023   Sunday   7:00 p.m.
Beth Jacob Congregation
9030 Olympic Boulevard   (Beverly Hills)
Tel. (213) 278-1911   Thursday   9:15 a.m.   (Women only)
Temple Beth Torah
225 South Atlantic Boulevard   (Alhambra)
Tel. (818) 284-0296   Monday 7:30 p.m.
Temple B'nai Emet
482 North Garfield Avenue   (Montebello)
Tel. (213) 723-2978   Wednesday   12:30 p.m.
Cafe Danssa (Dani Dassa)
11533 West Pico Boulevard   Tel. (213) 478-7866
   Sunday   8:30 - 12 midnight (Advanced session)
   Tuesday   8:45 - 12 midnight
   Thursday   8:30 - 12 midnight
   Saturday   8:45 - 12 midnight
Arthur Murray Dance Studio
6363 Van Nuys Avenue   Tel. (818) 785-5433   Sunday   8:00 p.m.
Congregation Shaarei Tefila
7269 Beverly Boulevard   Tel. (213) 938-7147
                     Thursday   1:15 p.m. (Women only)
Shaarey Zedek Congregation
12800 Chandler Boulevard   (North Holloywood)
Tel. (818) 763-0560   Tuesday   8:00 p.m.
Temple Solael
6601 Valley Circle Boulevard (San Fernando Valley)
Tel. (818) 348-3885   Monday   7:00 p.m.
University of Judaism
15600 Mulholland Drive (Bel Air)   Tel. (213) 879-411
                     Wednesday   7:30 - 10:30 p.m.
Valley Beth Shalom
15739 Ventura Boulevard   (Encino)   Tel. (818) 872-1360
   Wednesday   7:30 p.m.
   Friday - following services

Valley Cities JCC
13164 Burbank Boulevard   (Van Nuys)
Tel. (818) 786-6310
    Tuesday   8:00 p.m.
    Wednesday   7:30 p.m.
    Thursday   10:00 a.m.
    Saturday   8:30 p.m.

Westside JCC
5870 West Olympic Boulevard   Tel. (213) 938-2531
    Tuesday   9:00 a.m.
    Wednesday   7:30 p.m.

West Valley JCC
22622 Vanowen Street   (Canoga Park)   Tel. (818) 346-3003
    Tuesday   8:00 p.m.
    Wednesday   7:30 - 9:30 p.m.

Mountain View
Masonic Auditorium
890 Church Street   Tel. (415) 964-4277   Sunday   7 - 11:30 p.m.

Palo Alto
Palo Alto YWCA
4161 Alma Street   Tel. (415) 329-0465 or 328-6487
                              Thursday   8:30 - 11 p.m.

Dance with Mark
425 Hamilton (at Waverly)   Tel. (415) 249-4912

Pasadena   Friday   7:30 - 12 midnight

Pasadena Jewish Temple
1434 North Altadena Drive   Tel. (818) 798-1161   Tuesday   7:00 p.m.

San Francisco
San Francisco JCC
3200 California Street   Tel. (415) 346-6040 or 566-0896
    Monday   8:00-10:30 p.m.
    Saturday   8:00-12 midnight

Venice
Israel Levin Senior Center
201 Ocean Front Walk   Tel. (213) 399-9584   Tuesday   10:00 a.m.

Temple Mishkon Tephilo
206 Main Street   Tel. (213) 392-3029   Tuesday   8:15 p.m.
Walnut Creek   (East Bay)
Contra Costa JCC
2071 Tice Valley Boulevard   Tel. (415) 938-7800
                    Monday   7:30 p.m. (International folk dance)

ARIZONA
Phoenix
JCC of Greater Phoenix
1718 West Maryland Avenue   Tel. (602) 249-1832
                              Wednesday   7:00 - 11:00 p.m.

COLORADO
Denver
Temple Micah
2600 Leyden Street   Tel. (303) 388-4239   Tuesday   7:00 - 10 p.m.
Washington Park - Outdoor session   Summers - Thurday evenings

OREGON
Portland
Mittleman Jewish Community Center
6651 S.W. Capitol Highway   Tel. (503) 244-0111   Tuesday   7:00 p.m.

TEXAS
Houston
JCC of Houston   5601 South Breaswood   Tel. (713)729-3200
                              Thursday   8:00 p.m.
Congregation Beth Yeshurun
4525 Beechnut Boulevard   Tel. (713) 666-1881   Monday   8:00 p.m.

UTAH

Salt Lake City
Jewish Community Center
2416 East 1700 South   Tel. (801) 581-0098   Wednesday   7:30 p.m.

WASHINGTON

Seattle
Stroum Jewish Community Center
3801 East Mercer Way (Mercer Island)
Tel. (206) 232-7115   Wednesday   7:30 - 9:30 p.m.
Northend Branch (JCC)
8606 35th Avenue, NE   Tel. (206) 526-8073   Thursday   7:00 p.m.
Tacoma
Temple Beth El
5975 South 12 th Street   Tel. (206) 564-7101   Saturday   8:00 p.m.

CANADA

Vancouver, British Columbia
Vancouver JCC
950 West 41st Avenue   Tel. (604) 266-9111   Wednesday   8:30 - 10:30 p.m.
(Nona Malki   Tel. 522-2065)

JEWISH SINGLES SCENE

The following Jewish Community Centers offer special programs, dances and activities for Jewish singles of all age groups.

ARIZONA
Mesa 85202
JCC - Tri-City Branch   1720 West Southern, Suite C-6
Tel. (602) 962-0441
Phoenix 85015
JCC of Greater Phoenix   1718 West Maryland Avenue
Tel. (602) 249-1832
Scottsdale 85253
JCC - East Valley Branch
7119 East Shea Boulevard, Suite 101   Tel. (602) 998-9145
Tucson 85715
JCC of Tucson   3822 East River Drive   Tel. (602) 299-7933

CALIFORNIA
Berkeley 94709
JCC of Berkeley-Richmond   1414 Walnut
Tel. (415) 848-0237
Canoga Park 91307
West Valley JCC   22622 Vanowen Street Tel. (818) 346-3003
Carlsbad 92008
North County JCC   2725 Jefferson Street #8-B
Tel. (619) 729-5932
Granada Hills 91344
North Valley JCC   16601 Rinaldi Street   Tel. (818) 360-2211
Laguna Beach 92651
JCC of South Orange County   298 Broadway
Tel. (714) 497-2070

La Jolla   92037
North City JCC   8950 Villa La Jolla Drive, Suite 2131

Tel. (619) 460-9937

Long Beach   90815
JCC   3801 East Willow Avenue   Tel. (213) 426-7601

Los Angeles
Hollywood-Los Fez JCC   1110 Bates Avenue   (90029)

Tel. (213) 663-2255

Westside JCC   5870 West OLympic Boulevard   (90036)

Tel. (213) 938-2531

Oakland   94602
JCC of Oakland-Piedmont   3245 Sheffield Avenue

Tel. (415) 533-9222

Palm Springs   92262
JCC   611 South Canyon Drive   Tel. (619) 325-7281

Palo Alto   94303
South Peninsula JCC   830 East Meadow Drive

Tel. (415) 494-2511

Sacramento   95865
JCC   2351 Wyda Way   Tel. (916) 486-0906

San Diego   92111
JCC   7510 Clairemont, Mesa Boulevard   Tel. (619) 565-0280
JCC - College Area Branch   (92105)

4079 54th Street   Tel. (619) 583-3300

San Francisco   94132
Brotherhood Way Center   655 Brotherhood Way

Tel. (415) 334-7474

JCC   3200 California Street   (94118)   Tel. (415) 346-6040

San Jose   95125
JCC   2300 Canoas Garden Road   Tel. (408) 266-6317

San Rafael   94903
Marin JCC   200 North San Pedro Road   Tel. (415) 479-2000

Santa Monica   90404
Bay Cities JCC   2601 Santa Monica Boulevard

Tel. (213) 828-3433

Van Nuys 91401

Valley Cities JCC   13164 Burbank Boulevard

Tel. (818) 786-6310

Venice 90291

Israel Levin Senior Adult Center   201 Ocean Front Walk

Tel. (213) 399-9584

Walnut Creek 94596

Contra Costa JCC   1355 Creekside Drive   Tel. (415) 938-7800

COLORADO

Denver 80206

JCC of Denver   4800 Alameda Avenue   Tel. (303) 399-2660

OREGON

Portland 97219

Mittleman JCC   6651 S.W.Capitol Highway

Tel. (503) 244-0111

TEXAS

Dallas 75230

JCC of Dallas   7900 Northhaven Road   Tel. (214) 739-2737

El Paso 79912

405 Mardi Gras Drive   Tel. (915) 584-4438

Fort Worth 76133

JCC   6801 Granbury Road   Tel. (817) 292-3111

Houston 77096

JCC of Houston

5601 South Breaswood   Tel. (713) 729-3200

San Antonio 78216

JCC   103 West Rampart Drive   Tel. (512) 344-3453

UTAH

Salt Lake City 84108

JCC   2416 East 1700 South   Tel. (801) 581-0098

JEWISH SINGLES

WASHINGTON
Bremerton 99352
Jewish Community Center 11th & Veneta Tel. 1-373-9884
Seattle
Stroum JCC of Greater Washington
3801 East Mercer Way, Mercer Island (98040)
                                    Tel. (206) 232-7115
Bellevue Satellite 15749 N.E. 4th Street (98008)
                                    Tel. (206) 643-1495
Northend Branch 8606 35th Avenue, NE (98115)
                                    Tel. (206) 526-8073

CANADA
Vancouver, British Columbia V5Z 2N7
Vancouver JCC 950 West 41st Avenue Tel. (604) 266-9111

Bibliography

B'nai B'rith Messenger. Los Angeles, California

Brooks, J. *The History of the Jews of Utah & Idaho*.
  Salt Lake City: Western Epics, 1973

Cunin, Rabbi B.S. *Chabad - People Helping People 1965-1990*.
  Los Angeles: Chabad of California, 1990

Dreyfus, S. *Henry Cohen - Messenger of the Lord*.
  New York: Bloch Publishing, 1963

Family Resource Guide. Jewish Community Center of
  Denver

Greater Phoenix Jewish News. Phoenix, Arizona

Guide to the Jewish Community of Vancouver & British Columbia.
  Jewish Federation of Greater Vancouver, 1988

Gutkin, H. *Journey Into Our Heritage*. Toronto:
  Lester & Orpen Dennys, 1980

History of the Arizona Biltmore. Phoenix, Arizona

Hornbein, M. *Temple Emanu-El of Denver -
  A Centennial History*. Denver: A.B. Hirschfeld Press, 1974

Intermountain Jewish News. Denver, Colorado

Israelowitz, O. *Eat Your Way Through America & Canada*.
  New York: Israelowitz Publishing, 1990

The Jewish Calendar - Guide & Magazine. Canoga Park,
  California   February, 1991

The Jewish Journal of Greater Los Angeles. Los Angeles

The Jewish Reporter. Las Vegas, Nevada

The Jewish Review. Portland, Oregon

The Jewish Transcript. Seattle, Washington

Jewish Western Bulletin. Vancouver, British Columbia

Las Vegas Israelite. Las Vegas, Nevada

Lowenstein, S. *The Jews of Oregon 1850 - 1950*. Portland:
  Jewish Historical Society of Oregon, 1987

Magnin, Rabbi E.F. *The Warner Murals in the Wilshire Boulevard Temple.* Los Angeles: Wilshire Boulevard Temple, 1974

Northern California Jewish Bulletin. San Francisco

Ornish, N. *Pioneer Jewish Texans.* Dallas, Texas. Texas Heritage Press, 1989

Pioneer Jews of Arizona 1850-1920. (Video) Phoenix: Plotkin Judaica Museum, 1988

Postal, B. & Koppman, L. *American Jewish Landmarks - A Travel Guide & History.* New York: Fleet Press, 1986

Resource Book. San Francisco Jewish Federation

Rochlin, H. & F. *Pioneer Jews - A New Life in the Far West.* Boston: Houghton Mifflin Co., 1984

Sass, S.J. *Jewish Los Angeles - A Guide.* Los Angeles: Jewish Federation of Greater Los Angeles, 1982

Tigay, A.M. *The Jewish Traveler.* Garden City: Doubleday & Company, 1987

Wishnitzer, R. Synagogues of the United States. Philadelphia: The Jewish Publication Society of America, 1955

Catalog

GUIDE TO JEWISH N. Y.C.
by Oscar Israelowitz
ISBN 1-878741-00-4 $9.95

GUIDE TO JEWISH ITALY
by Annie Sacerdoti
ISBN 0-9611036-3-9 $12.95

GUIDE TO JEWISH EUROPE
Western Europe - 7th Edition
by Oscar Israelowitz
ISBN 1-878741-05-5 $11.95

GUIDE TO THE JEWISH WEST
by Oscar Israelowitz
ISBN 1-878741-06-3 $11.95

GUIDE TO JEWISH CANADA & U.S.A.
Volume I - Eastern Provinces
by Oscar Israelowitz
ISBN 0-9611036-8-X $11.95

ELLIS ISLAND GUIDE WITH LOWER MANHATTAN
by Oscar Israelowitz
ISBN 1-878741-01-2 $7.95

EAT YOUR WAY THROUGH AMERICA & CANADA
A Kosher Dining Guide
by Oscar Israelowitz
ISBN 1-878741-03-9 $5.95

GUIDE TO JEWISH U.S.A.
Volume II - South
by Oscar Israelowitz
ISBN 0-9611036-6-3 $9.95

LOWER EAST SIDE GUIDE
4th Edition
by Oscar Israelowitz
ISBN 1-878741-04-7 $6.95

N. Y.C. SUBWAY GUIDE
by Oscar Israelowitz
ISBN 0-9611036-7-1 $6.95

FLATBUSH GUIDE
by Oscar Israelowitz
ISBN 0-9611036-9-8 $4.95

201 YIDDISH VERBS
by Anna Rockowitz
ISBN 0-8120-0604-6 $9.95

BOROUGH PARK GUIDE
by Oscar Israelowitz
ISBN 0-9611036-2-0 $2.95

Israelowitz Publishing

P.O.Box 228 Brooklyn, New York 11229   Tel. (718) 951-7072

Biography

Oscar Israelowitz was born in Brussels, Belgium. He is an architectural consultant by profession. Some of his projects include the Synagogue and Holocaust Center of the Bobover chassidim in Borough Park and the Yeshiva Rabbi Chaim Berlin (both in Brooklyn, New York). He has also designed homes and villas for clients in the United States, Haiti and Israel.

Mr. Israelowitz is also a professional photographer. His works have been on exhibit in the Whitney Museum of American Art, the Brooklyn Museum, the Long Island (now Brooklyn) Historical Society and Yeshiva University Museum. One of his exhibits is on permanent display in the New York Transit Museum.

Oscar Israelowitz has appeared on several television and radio programs including the *Joe Franklin Show*, NBC's *First Estate - Religion in Review* and Ruth Jacob's *Jewish Home Show.*

In more recent years, Mr. Israelowitz has been conducting weekly tours of Ellis Island and the Lower East Side. These tours have been written-up in *New York Magazine,* the *Washington Post,* the *Los Angeles Times* and the *Chicago Tribune.*

Index

NOTES

NOTES

NOTES

DATE DUE